A Clinic

for

Dirty Divas

Coming Clean on Sexy Stains and Messes

LAURA GOODMAN

Lago Press
Owings Mills, Maryland

Copyright © 2005 Laura Goodman

All rights reserved. No part of this book may be reproduced or transmitted in any form or by any means, electronic or mechanical, including photocopying, recording, or by any information storage and retrieval system, without permission in writing from the publisher.

Published by Lago Press
Owings Mills, Maryland 21117

Publisher's Cataloging-in-Publication Data
Goodman, Laura.
A cleaning manual for Dirty Divas : coming clean on sexy stains and messes / Laura Goodman. – Owings Mills, MD : Lago Press, c2005.

p. ; cm.
ISBN 10: 0-9772476-0-0
ISBN 13: 978-0-9772476-0-8

1. Spotting (Cleaning)-Handbooks, manuals, etc. 2. Cleaning-Handbooks, manuals, etc. 3. Laundry-Handbooks, manuals, etc. I. Title.

TX324 .G66 2005
648/.5-dc22   2005932987

Book production and coordination by Jenkins Group, Inc.
www.bookpublishing.com
Interior design by Chris Rhoads and Debbie Sidman
Cover design by Chris Rhoads
Cover and interior illustrations by Jenniffer Julich

Printed in the United States of America
09 08 07 06 05 • 5 4 3 2 1

This book is dedicated to all the Dirty Divas I know, including DaDa, Amber, Gail, Kat, Rebecca, Nina, Susan, Jessica, and Jayne. They know what a Dirty Diva I am and still love me despite it. This is also dedicated to my family, but heaven forbid, if you are a family member, close the bloody book now.

CONTENTS

CHAPTER ONE
Introduction 1

CHAPTER TWO
What Is a Dirty Diva? 9

CHAPTER THREE
Sex-Stain Removers 13

- 1) Acetone 13
- 2) Alcohol (rubbing) 13
- 3) Ammonia 13
- 4) Baking soda 14
- 5) Canola oil 14
- 6) Club soda 14

7) Cornstarch	14
8) Denture tablets	14
9) Dishwashing detergent	14
10) Glass cleaner	14
11) Goo Gone	14
12) Hydrogen peroxide	14
13) Laundry detergent	14
14) Lemon juice	14
15) Makeup remover	15
16) Meat tenderizer	15
17) Nail polish remover	15
18) Peanut butter	15
19) Salt	15
20) Shampoo	15
21) Toothpaste	15
22) Turpentine	15
23) Vinegar	15
24) White wine	15

CHAPTER FOUR

Materials 17

1) Acetate	18
2) Acrylic	18
3) Angora	18
4) Bathing suits	19
5) Cashmere	20

CONTENTS

6)	Chiffon	21
7)	Corduroy	21
8)	Cotton	22
9)	Denim	23
10)	Down	24
11)	Feathers	24
12)	Flannel	24
13)	Fur	25
14)	Glass	26
15)	Lace	28
16)	Leather	29
17)	Linen	30
18)	Metal	31
19)	Mohair	32
20)	Nylon	33
21)	Plastic	33
22)	Polyester	34
23)	Rayon	35
24)	Satin	35
25)	Silk	36
26)	Spandex	37
27)	Stone	38
28)	Suede	39
29)	Velour/Velvet	40
30)	Wood	40
31)	Wool	41

CHAPTER FIVE
Sex-Induced Stains 43

   1) Antiperspirant/Deodorant 44
   2) Body fluids 44
      a) Blood 44
      b) Fecal matter 46
      c) Perspiration 48
      d) Semen/Feminine moisture 49
      e) Urine 50
      f) Vomit 51
   3) Burn marks 52
   4) Food/Drink 54
      a) Alcoholic beverages 54
      b) Butter/Margarine 56
      c) Chocolate/Chocolate syrup 57
      d) Fruit/Fruit juice 58
      e) Gum 59
      f) Ice cream 61
      g) Jell-O 62
      h) Mayonnaise 63
      i) Mustard 64
      j) Oil/Grease 65
      k) Syrup 67
      l) Tomato 68
      m) Whipped cream 69
      n) Wine 71
   5) Grass/Flowers 73
   6) Hair 73

CONTENTS

7) Ink	74
8) Lubes	75
9) Makeup	76
a) Blush, eyeliner, eye shadow, foundation, and mascara	76
b) Lipstick	77
c) Nail polish	79
10) Mud/Dirt	80
11) Odors	81
12) Oil/Grease	82
13) Paint	82
14) Soot	83
15) Tree sap	84
16) Wax	84
17) Wood/Furniture polish	86

CHAPTER SIX
Closing   **89**

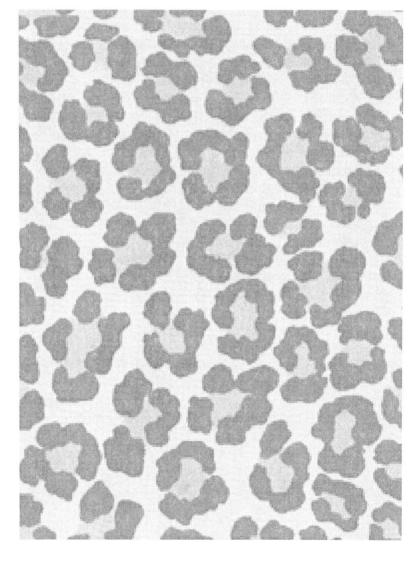

1

INTRODUCTION

SO YOU WAKE UP to find that the guy you just slept with is gone, and the only thing you have to remember him by is the cum stain on your brand new feather-cuffed shirt. Then, three weeks later, you get so drunk at a social event that you're heaving into the toilet of an elite hotel bathroom. You somehow manage to miss the toilet completely but are able to thoroughly saturate your gorgeous Jones

New York suede stilettos in your chunks. And who could forget your surreptitious stuff session with that guy in the back of his SUV? He says that people still ask him how those footprints got on his back windshield. Don't ask me—you can figure it out on your own.

Okay, so these occurrences are not the norm, but they do happen. In fact, these little mishaps occur all the time—in every bedroom, hotel, and SUV in the country. They happen in every train, hot tub, and zoo (yes, zoo) in the world! They're going on as you read this introduction! If these unfortunate little accidents don't happen to everyone all the time, they sure do happen to me—*all* the time. I also suspect that although you may not be willing to readily admit it, you and many other like-minded women experience these follies as well.

I seem to attract sex-induced stains. I've found them on the feathered cuffs of my brand new shirt, my good black pants, my expensive silk sheets, my carpet, my wall, and perhaps the strangest place of all, in my jewelry. These are not just semen stains either. They consist of everything from burn marks to bad odors. Let me tell you, there's nothing like trying to get tree sap out of your spandex leggings.

A girl could really get a complex about attracting all these unusual messes. But I soon realized that there should always be something to clean up after sexual relations. If nothing's broken or soiled afterwards, then something's not being done right. After coming to that realization, I'm now complex free.

I was finally inspired to write this book soon after one of my girlfriends came to visit me. We were in my bedroom and, as usual, most of my clothes were on the floor. Lifting my famed feather-cuffed shirt,

INTRODUCTION

I joked to my friend that this was the "Fred" shirt. I then pointed to my "Josh" pants, informing her that he considerately demonstrated his affection for me on them for everyone to see. I had the clothes divided up into groups. Lights. Darks. Cold cycle. Warm cycle. Hand wash. Dry-clean only. Dry-clean was divided into two piles: one was the normal-wear-and-tear pile, and the other was the unusual-stains-you-dread-telling-your-dry-cleaner-about pile.

For some reason, I couldn't bear telling that nice, smiling little Asian dry cleaner that he was holding last night's flavor in his hand. The funny part is, I had no problem telling my podiatrist that I thought the reason I had gotten a fungal infection on my feet was because my then boyfriend sucked my toes every day due to his foot fetish. The podiatrist prescribed an antifungal cream for my feet and discouraged me from allowing my boyfriend to suck the medication off my toes! Why was I okay with divulging embarrassing information to the doctor and not my dry cleaner?

Soon I realized why I was so uncomfortable confessing my sex-stained secrets to my dry cleaner. While my doctor was responsible for my health, my dry cleaner wasn't. My podiatrist knew he risked catching an infection or a disease from his patients—risks that are universally acknowledged as part of his job. He was informed, so he took precautions. He may have been secretly shocked by my deviant divulgence, but his job was to keep me healthy. The dry cleaner, however, didn't intend to take on the responsibility of curing people of infection and disease; his sole purpose was just to make sure society's clothes were pressed and smelled nice. Knowing he's handling some guy's jizz stain isn't a burden a dry cleaner should have to bear.

Back in my bedroom, my friend and I arranged some pillows and got comfortable. We bonded by my friend's cooing over her husband and son and I, being the single friend, regaled her with my make-out stories. I explained to her that my make-out sessions come in waves. Sometimes, there are no treats for months on end. Other times, my opportunities are so numerous that I can't keep the names and conversations straight (I prefer the latter). My friend always wants to know the dirty details, so I give them to her. She'll ask, "How did it feel?" or "How big is his dick?" I'll respond with, "Great," or "It was so massive, I thought I wouldn't get out alive." We really get down to the nitty-gritty.

After wrapping up our girlfriend gab session, the conversation floated back to laundry. I asked her, "Seriously, should I take these to my dry cleaner without telling him what the stains are?" Ethically, I feel he should know that he's about to handle splooge or vomit. What if he wants to take precautions? If any of my loved ones were to become dry cleaners, I wouldn't want them unwittingly catching god-knows-what from managing cum-stained garments. My friend assured me that all dry cleaners know they'll sometimes get garments with "those kinds" of stains on them. I said, "What a shame they don't teach 'How to Clean Semen Stains' in home economics!"

INTRODUCTION

Shortly following the day my girlfriend and I spent together, I was involved in yet another fateful boffing blunder involving copier toner and my white silk pants. Between conversations about sex-induced stains with my girlfriend and having to clean copier ink from my pants, I found myself asking, "Whom am I supposed to approach for advice on cleaning all these unusual messes? Whomever I ask would naturally want to know how these mystery stains occurred." I pontificated further. "There are tons of books on cleaning, but none on this 'special' type of cleaning. I just wish there were a book on the kind of cleaning that 'active' divas have to do." Then it hit me. I could become the expert, and my fellow "Dirty Divas" could gain knowledge by using my writing as their resource! At that moment, I realized I needed to take it upon myself to educate other women who may have been feeling equally as frustrated.

Immediately, I put pen to paper and began to record situations in which sex-induced stains would ruin otherwise beautiful garments or materials. The words seemed to flow from my head to my hand. Effortlessly, I was able to compile multiple scenarios with which other Dirty Divas would be familiar. Once my work was finished, I read over its contents. I was filled with such a strong feeling of reassurance that it could have only resulted from realizing that I now had an explicit reference to address my questions. Up to that point I had always been answered obscurely. I came to understand that by not publishing this book, I was actually withholding information that other women in my situation desperately needed to know. It was then that I decided to make this book accessible so that others could, like I had, take comfort in the fact that they could accurately inform themselves while maintaining a pristine wardrobe, car, etc.

I hereby bequeath to you this guide as evidence of the fact that you are not alone in your struggles to clean sex-induced messes. So, take heed, Dirty Divas, and embrace the teachings in this book. Know that another DD has experienced what you are going through right now. I pray that you are liberated after gaining the ability to properly clean, with confidence and without hesitation, your or your lover's mess. I dream that you can hold your head high with the knowledge that you are able to take care of any untidiness that may come your way. Most important, I hope that you will be proud of the fact that you did all of this without asking for help from your dry cleaner.

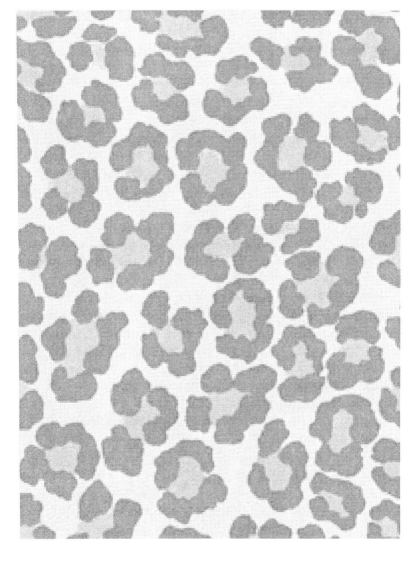

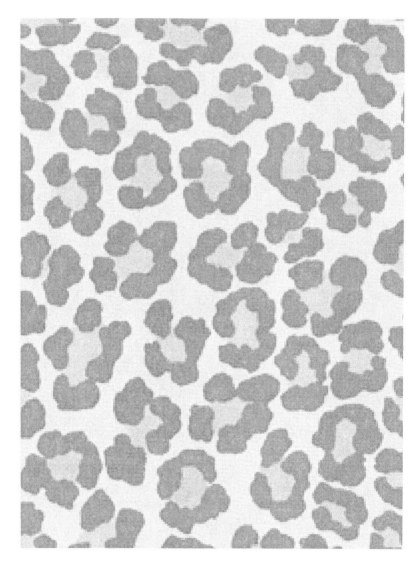

2

WHAT IS A DIRTY DIVA?

A DIRTY DIVA IS ANY woman or she-man who is unapologetic about her desire for and execution of sexual acts. She feels empowered by her sexuality and sees nothing wrong with using it to her full advantage. A DD may be kinky or not, but whatever her tastes, she never fails to respect others' choices (unless they're nonconsensual). She also knows that although she is candid about her sexual experiences, others are sometimes not, so she is careful not to offend them.

The DD has a tendency to do very dirty things, and she can't fight her inclinations—they're too deeply rooted in her psyche. She does know, however, that not everyone shares her preferences. Thus she is cognizant of respecting those who don't. As a result, she'll often take the position that she should not be the "moral police" to others—her motto is "To each her own." Basically, if the Dirty Diva learns that you enjoy getting blindfolded and tied to a bed while your lover calls you "Mommy," even if her tastes are different, she'll always respect your right to do whatever you want in the privacy of your own home (hotel room/alleyway).

Usually, a Dirty Diva also has a somewhat "manly" quality in that she is able to effectively separate sex and love. This ability causes the mandatory "waiting period" before sexual contact with another to be pure torture for the excitable Dirty Diva. In fact, if she were a Miss America contestant, she wouldn't wish for world peace (impossible); she'd wish that sexually impulsive women would still be respected in the morning (improbable).

Although she will conform to the rules to get what she wants, many of the men she meets are not able to do the same. By definition, the Dirty Diva is never apologetic about her sexual acts or desires because she has no reason to be; she is always forthright and never leaves things unresolved. Unlike the typical man, she will directly inform the person she no longer wishes to see of her intentions. She wouldn't just stop calling him (or her), give him lame excuses for not setting a date, or convey false hope of a future date if she's not interested. She doesn't toy with others' emotions because she knows that she would want to be treated with dignity and respect if she were to fall for someone who was not romantically interested in her. As a result of this enlightenment, the Dirty Diva never leads a man on a futile search because she is not a tease. If she talks the talk, she'll walk the one-eye. Of course, teasing can be fun, but only if it's followed with action.

Basically, the Dirty Diva follows the letter of the law when it comes to love, but when it comes time to play, she breaks all the rules.

Finally, although the Dirty Diva loves to get down with the get down, she can't stand to live in squalor. She knows that she must practice self-respect by keeping her surroundings in good order because she realizes that she outwardly projects to the world anything that she is inwardly feeling. She would never want to indicate that she is not in complete control of her life. By keeping her environment clean and orderly, she demonstrates that she is the only one in charge of her own life.

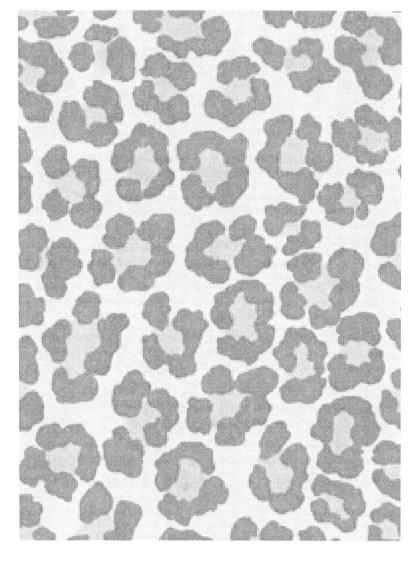

3

SEX-STAIN REMOVERS

IRTY DIVAS SHOULD HAVE the following materials on hand:

*1) **Acetone:*** Very strong. Take care when using on clothes and plastics. Keep away from your fireplace down below.

*2) **Alcohol (rubbing):*** Not the kind you drink. Use to remove stains and disinfect.

*3) **Ammonia:*** Don't use on grass stains, even the ones you got on your pants while you were getting the hole in one on the golf course.

4) **Baking soda:** Ideal for removing odors (morning pussy) from clothes and for removing stains that require absorption.

5) **Canola oil:** It basically "re-oils" stains so you can remove them. Use any excess for hand jobs.

6) **Club soda:** Mild. Use on almost any surface or material. It's also good for a hangover.

7) **Cornstarch:** Great for drawing the moisture and oil out of a stain, sort of like the way your mouth works on a cream jug.

8) **Denture tablets:** Steal some from your sugar daddy's medicine cabinet. They're great stain removers for white items!

9) **Dishwashing detergent (liquid):** Terrific for cutting grease on any oily mess you or your lover may produce.

10) **Glass cleaner:** Mirror, mirror on the wall, who's the dirtiest diva of them all?

11) **Goo Gone:** Not man goo—household goo. It's also a great wax remover.

12) **Hydrogen peroxide:** Use 3% (the kind you use for cuts) on the stains you get on your sheets when you're flagging and your lover has parted your red sea.

13) **Laundry detergent (liquid and cold-water formula):** Unmatched for pretreating jizz stains.

14) **Lemon juice:** Fantastic for bleaching your clothes or your lower wig. Apply to your fluff, and sunbathe bottomless until blond. Don't try with conventional bleach!

*15) **Makeup remover (nonoily):*** Best for removing ... makeup. Duh!

*16) **Meat tenderizer (unseasoned):*** Perfect for removing blood, cum, and ice cream stains.

*17) **Nail polish remover (nonacetone):*** Ideal for stripping ... nail polish. No need to get your mind out of the gutter, just make a little room for me!

*18) **Peanut butter (smooth, not chunky):*** In lieu of cock or gash, gum is great for satisfying an oral fixation. You don't, however, want it stuck to your bra! PB removes gum.

*19) **Salt:*** Good for deterring red wine stains. It's also good on the rim ... of a margarita.

*20) **Shampoo:*** Excellent for removing oily stains and washing a sexy someone's hair (during the first date, of course).

*21) **Toothpaste (regular/nongel):*** Fights stains on sturdy fabrics. Use, for example, on the knees of your jeans.

*22) **Turpentine:*** Removes paint. I know you're expecting some kind of clever remark from me, but I've got nothing. Turpentine is just not sexy!

*23) **Vinegar (white):*** Great for various stains, including stains on suede. Use excess to toss your salad.

*24) **White wine:*** Excellent for removing red wine stains. Who are we kidding; we just want an excuse to drink more.

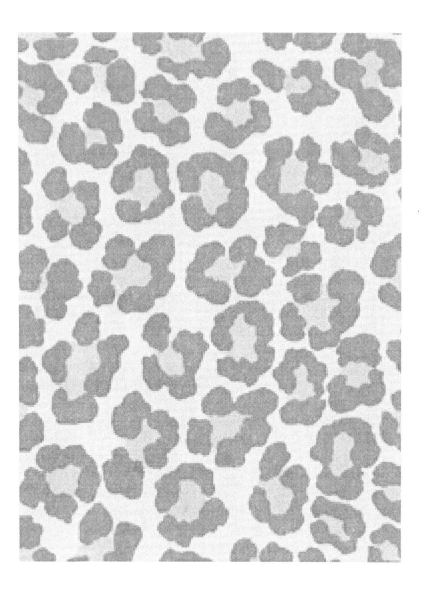

4

MATERIALS

A DIRTY DIVA CAN AND will attract stains on her clothes and personal belongings. The following section describes the different types of materials that a DD may need to clean during the course of her sex life. Every fabric and material is different, so **you must follow the directions on your garments' labels before consulting the following section.**

1) Acetate: Imagine yourself wearing plastic wrap all over your body (just like last night with Scott). If you had to take off that plastic wrap and clean it, you wouldn't throw it into a hot washing machine for fear it would melt. Acetate is basically a plastic, so you have to be very careful about how you clean it.

The best way to clean acetate is to machine or hand wash it in cold water. As long as you don't wring out the garment, you shouldn't get too many wrinkles. If you did a little too much bumping and grinding with Scotty boy, then use a cool iron on the very lowest setting; otherwise, you'll see shiny marks (spots of melted material) all over your garment.

2) Acrylic: Now, imagine yourself wearing plastic wrap containing real bits of cloth (like a Britney Spears costume). Most acrylic blends come this way.

Basically, follow the directions for acetate, except make sure to wash acrylic more frequently. Acrylic will hold some funky odors if not freshened regularly. Can you say "smelly girl"?

3) Angora: Ooh, angora. I love angora. I love to wear it because its fuzziness tones down this Dirty Diva's sometimes intimidating demeanor. Wearing white angora will give even the naughtiest girl the air of innocence. Angora is so heavenly because it's made from rabbit fur—that's right, little bunnies. Unless you're a vegetarian, you'll get over it.

Of course, my favorite piece is my wine-colored angora sweater. Why? If I'm at a party and spill my fourth merlot on it, I don't go into a panic. For the sake of any spectators at the scene, I just pretend that my high heel got caught in something on the floor, even though I was really just trying to check the time on my watch and forgot that I had a glass of wine in my hand. Afterwards, I don't have to worry about drawing even more attention to myself by having to clean a large stain out of my sweater. I can just blot and mingle because the color of the merlot effortlessly blends into the wine-tinted fabric. When the next cute guy comes along, not noticing anything amiss, he'll think I look great. (Of course, I'll probably smell like I live out of a cardboard box.)

The most effective way to clean angora is to hand wash it in cold water with only a little liquid laundry detergent. Just as with any delicate fabric, you can't twist. Don't rub either (save the rubbing for your boss on "raise" day) because the fuzziness will rub away, leaving you with less garment. Push and press out the moisture as best you can, and then dry flat. If you're left with wrinkles, take your crumpled ass to the gym steam room, and allow the steam to plump your ass and your garment. However, a steamy iron (don't actually touch the iron to the fabric) is much more effective and convenient.

4) ***Bathing suits:*** Anything having to do with wet, hard, barely dressed bodies is sexy. The only thing sexier is actual sex. Alas, sex is not allowed on the coastline! Bathing suits will just have to suffice until we are allowed to boink boisterously on the beach. A Dirty Diva chooses her bathing suit like a soldier chooses a weapon. Because there's a lot of competition out there, she has to be the one to garner the most attention. She plays dirty because she is dirty. How did one Dirty Diva foul her beautiful new suit? Well, the lifeguard on duty felt it was his duty to introduce her to his electric eel. As it turned out, the introductions took place right on top of an opened bottle of suntan lotion. What a creamy mess!

Whether you've been swimming in the ocean or the pool, you must keep your suit clean to prolong its life. If you're visiting the shore, go back to your hotel room after you've finished swimming. Allow the maid to turn down your bed and remove your bathing suit. After she's cleaned your cubby, place your bathing suit in cool water for about five minutes. Using gentle laundry detergent (even face soap will do), hand wash your suit. Rinse, and lay flat to dry. Finally, spread legs, and lay flat while you wait for the maid to come back.

5) *Cashmere*: Cashmere is the cornerstone fabric in the wardrobe of the Dirty Diva. If you own cashmere, either you have very good taste or your Uncle Teddy drives women into the Chappaquiddick. Angora and cashmere are very similar in that both are fuzzy, soft materials deriving from animals. Angora : rabbits :: cashmere : goats. Cashmere comes from a cashmere goat. Quick test ... where does cashmere come from? Cashmere comes from goats. Weren't you listening? I know you spend most of your time perfecting your blow job technique or figuring out the exact location of your girlfriend's G-spot, but come on, we're learning how to clean, people!

Where were we? Oh, yeah, cashmere. Hopefully, you won't smear dark black mascara on your light pink cashmere when you're taking it off for Danny, but just in case ...

Dry-clean only. Remember the piles of clothes on my bedroom floor? Even though I'm a Dirty Diva, I must make sure my clothes are clean. If you're going to spend a hundred dollars or more on a freakin' sweater, then just spend the money to get it dry-cleaned. If you have to wash your cashmere yourself, then do so in the same manner you would angora, except use liquid soap that doesn't lather. If you get a lot of lather, you'll have to manipulate (like what you did to yourself in the back row of the movie theater) the fabric too much, causing the garment to wear away. Despite being a Dirty Diva, you should not wear peekaboo cashmere unless you're walking down the red carpet.

6) ***Chiffon (also see "Silk"):*** If you happen to be wearing chiffon, perhaps to an evening event or as part of a wicked ensemble to drive your lover crazy, then you've got to learn how to clean it. After all, escargot is not the only thing that can ooze onto your garment!

7) ***Corduroy:*** This fabric is not an especially favorite one for Dirty Divas. Let's face it, so many more materials scream "sex kitten" rather than groan "college professor." College professor—maybe

there's something sexy about it after all! The love juice stain on his pants, however, must be removed.

Turn the garment inside out (so it doesn't accumulate lint from other garments), and toss it in the warm water cycle. Tumble dry on low. The key to avoid major wrinkles is taking the garment out of the dryer before it is completely dry and smoothing the pattern. Allow the garment to finish drying naturally and, if you need to, iron the garment inside out. Smooth the corduroy fibers with a lint brush (not roller).

By the way, the sound of someone walking in corduroy mimics the sound of crickets about to copulate. Doesn't that get you hot?

*8) **Cotton:*** Dirty Divas love to don innocent looking white cotton panties. They have a way of making a woman feel like a schoolgirl, and that's very dirty when you're makin' it with your full-grown man (or woman). I have a pair of white cotton panties with the word "jailbait" on them. Doesn't that sound bad? I wore the scandalous panties the night I met Officer Dave. After he noticed the felonious phrase on my underwear, he promptly detained me and read me my rights. He explained that I had the right to remain silent but that moaning was always encouraged. Dave also told me that anything I said or did would be held against me. Incidentally, I said and did nothing, but he proceeded to hold it against me anyway. When I got foundation on Dave's cotton boxers, I took care of it right away.

Remember that lights go with lights and darks go with darks. Cotton acts like a sponge for dyes. When you put a bright-red sock in with a load of whites, everything will come out pink except the sock, which will remain annoyingly red. If you were to put that red sock in with a load of darks, you wouldn't care if the red bled onto anything else because you wouldn't be able to tell.

An important fact about cotton is that it is very prone to shrinking. If you don't have the abs to pull off a skintight baby tee, then put your garments in the dryer on a low setting, remove them before they are completely dry, and smooth them with a hot iron.

9) *Denim:* Do you like flaunting camel toe? Then chances are you also have a mullet. There's nothing that screams "trailer trash" more than a bad case of camel toe. Some guys say they like to see the outline of a nice, juicy snatch in a tight pair of jeans, but these are usually the same guys who've papered their bedroom walls with Iron Maiden posters. If your guy likes camel toe, keep it in the bedroom (away from civilized society), and be sure to wash your jeans in very, very hot water and tumble dry on high.

For those who like unleavened bread, machine wash in warm water. I like to toss my jeans in the dryer for a little bit, but just like with cotton, I take them out while still damp to allow them to finish drying naturally. If you're on a low-carb diet and are losing weight, put your jeans in the dryer without any worries. Fuck you! May someone slip sugar into your bacon and eggs!

10) *Down (also see "Feathers")*: When I go for a romp on my heavenly down-filled bed, accidents always occur. The down serves as a cushion to protect my body during overzealous pleasure sessions, but I invariably see (or feel) gooey messes afterwards.

Put your down comforter or pillow in the washing machine, and obey the washing instructions for the outer covering of the down. Tumble dry on low. Some people like to add tennis balls to the drying cycle, but whatever you do, don't add racquetballs. Number one, they're harder (they'll fuck up your dryer). Number two, they're usually blue. What's worse than a fucked up dryer with blue balls?

11) *Feathers*: If you are a good Dirty Diva, you've read my introduction to this book. Thus, you know that I was the unfortunate slut who discovered snake foam on her feather-cuffed shirt. I was more pissed about the foam on my shirt than the fact that the bastard never called me after the deed. In the '20s, flappers donned feathers galore. Feathers are sexy in the same way as angora or cashmere. They provide a woman or cross-dresser with a softer, more feminine or angelic quality.

To clean feathers, gently run them under lukewarm water. Then, stroke a very gentle liquid cleanser (face cleanser is fine) through the feathers. Gently pat the feathers dry with a clean, dry towel. Finally, allow them to thoroughly air dry before fluffing gently with your fingers.

12) *Flannel*: I really hope you're reading this part only because you need to get tree sap out of your lumberjack boyfriend's (or

MATERIALS

girlfriend's) shirt. A Dirty Diva does not usually wear flannel. How did you get that tree sap stain anyway? Probably the same way I did (bumping uglies against a tree in the woods).

Treat flannel like you would cotton.

13) *Fur:* I'm referring not to your nappy nugget but to the coat you wore to the latest showing of *The Producers*. Fur is by far the most expensive of all garments, and there's a reason Hollywood starlets will pay upwards of $30,000 for a mere coat. Fashioning fur pieces is very time consuming and costly. For manufacturers, the cost is a monetary one, but for animals, the cost is life.

Although I own some fur items (passed down from my grandmother), I get upset when I think about all the innocent animals slaughtered for nothing but a goddamn coat. By the same token, I should get upset when I put on a pair of leather shoes or eat a McChicken sandwich, but I don't. That makes me a hypocrite. My point (lacking any moral impact whatsoever) is if you truly want to wear fur, don't think about it; just wear it! (If you're ready to battle hypocrisy, send donations to the ADL.)

Humankind has worn fur for as long as it has been in existence. Before modern civilization, cavemen strategically placed fur cloths over their loins to conceal their shortcomings. Now, wearing fur is sexually titillating for many people. Trent Reznor from Nine Inch Nails echoes my point best when he sings "I want to fuck you like an animal!"

Men and women project different images when wearing fur. (The following information does not apply to our bean-flicking sisters or our pickle-kissing brothers.) For a woman, wearing fur signifies that other men had better steer clear because she is already taken by a "big, strong, savage man"—even if that man is of troll-like stature with hair plugs and an irrational fear of chickens. (What a woman won't do for fur!) On the other hand, a man proving his strength and virility implies that he can and will fight to kill for his family's survival, and he wears his fur as his trophy. Let's venture out of Bedrock now, shall we?

Fur responds best to professional cleaning. If you can afford to own it, you should budget cleaning into the equation. If you just need to freshen your fur garment, you should brush baking soda into the fusty areas and shake clean.

14) Glass: There will be three reasons you'll need to clean glass. First, you'll need to clean the fog off the car windows after you and Steve get it on. Second, you and a certain sex enthusiast may have broken his expensive art deco vase after he forced you onto his black lacquer coffee table and penetrated you in ways you've never thought possible (not that I would know anything about that). Finally, if you happen to be a "scratcher," you may have inadvertently gouged a glass-top table during a secret rendezvous with your best friend's brother. Remember, Dirty Divas always need to clean up after romps; otherwise, they're not doing it right.

To get windows sparkling, soak a clean, lint-free rag in a little vinegar and rub the glass in a circular motion. This

MATERIALS

technique also works for footprints on the mirrored wall behind your lover's bed.

Cleaning broken glass is the trickiest of all. As you're bopping your way around the house, things can get out of hand, and before you know it, glass is broken on the floor. If the glass happens to break during your love fest, first, take care of what you and your lover started in another location. (Nothing sucks more than having to throw water on the fires of passion, even if it is just a quickie.) Once both of you have gotten your Jones' off, go back to the scene of the hit-and-run (you can let your clumsy meathead fall asleep). If the glass was broken on a hard surface, first carefully pick up any large shards, and then vacuum where you see any tiny bits. You must be overly cautious and vacuum even where you think the glass could not have traveled. (When glass breaks, there's no rhyme or reason to where it lands.) Once you've finished sucking up (ooh!) every last bit, slightly moisten a paper towel with some water and swipe the entire vacuumed area. Be sure to use a paper towel because if you use a cloth towel, you'll get glass splinters in your hands when you wring it out. You can't swipe the area enough. Pay special attention to any grouted/grooved areas that act as cradles for invisible pieces of glass. Discard the paper towels when finished. After regrouting me and my bathroom tiles a couple of years ago, Rich accidentally knocked my bottle of Samsara perfume onto the ceramic-tiled floor. I was forced to learn the aforementioned cleaning trick because, even though I swept up the broken glass, I was getting splinters in my feet for months to come—painful reminders of the not-so-glass-shattering encounter.

Hopefully, if you broke glass, you broke it on a carpeted surface. Even if there are any small pieces left over after vacuuming, less injury will occur because any random pieces of glass will likely fall below the surface of the carpet where they cannot make contact with your skin. Broken glass on a hard surface is a more dangerous situation because the glass has nowhere to go but in your foot, hand, ass, etc. The most important thing to remember about cleaning broken glass is that thoroughness is the key. Nothing says "bummer" more than having to pull a shard of sharp stuff out of your booty when you are ready to climax.

Okay, Catwoman, so you've managed to scratch a glass-top coffee table? This only works for fine scratches, so trim your funky-ass acrylic fingernails. Then, rub some regular toothpaste into the etchings on the glass, and gently buff away.

15) *Lace*: This is a favorite fabric for a Dirty Diva. Lace is always sexy. You can see through where you shouldn't and can't where you should. Very *tit*illating! When your boyfriend gratifies himself between your breasts and ruins your new lacy bustier, take action on the stain immediately after he drifts off to sleep.

Most people agree that lace should be safety pinned to a sturdy towel before hand washing in lukewarm water. Lace is very delicate, so avoid twisting or rubbing. Smooth the lace onto a clean, dry towel to dry. Note: a bustier/bra contains metal stays, so you may omit the step that requires attaching the material to a towel.

16) *Leather (also see "Suede")*: The smell of leather is so intoxicating. Whenever I'm getting my leather stretched by a man in his leather-upholstered car, I think of my very first boyfriend (sorry, no names for this one). He smelled so good in his leather jacket. Then, I immediately go to the "Cotton" section in this book because I need to clean my panties (if I'm actually wearing them at the time). I literally start to salivate when I smell something that reminds me of him—those eyes, that body! Oh my God, the body ... give me a minute ... okay, all better!

Not too long ago, I got involved with a man who really enjoyed getting whipped, and whips are generally made of leather. The use of leather has transcended the clothing and auto industries to the sexual products market. Maybe we become so animalistic once exposed to it because leather comes from animals. Some enlightened couples have even fashioned the headboards behind their beds from this supple material. A love nest made of leather? Two words: Yum-my!

Leather is best treated with leather cleaner bought from a store that specializes in leather goods. Leather cleaner is more effective than other cleaners because it contains emollients that keep your leather healthy. If you have a stained item (your lover's leather chaps), apply the cleaner directly to the stain, allow it to penetrate for five to 10 minutes, and then clean the area with a rubbing motion. Finally, wipe away all excess cleaner.

Although this is not encouraged, I have also cleaned leather with regular soap and water. I dampened a washcloth, applied soap to the cloth, and gently rubbed the stain clean. Next, I used a soap-free, damp cloth to wipe the freshly cleansed area free of any remaining soap and thoroughly dried the area with a dry cloth. If you choose to use the soap-and-water method, make sure you condition the leather after cleaning. You can spray a small amount of cooking oil or leave-in hair conditioner (alcohol-free) on a soft cloth and buff until absorbed.

If you take your item to the cleaners, make sure when you pick it up to remove the plastic covering that has been placed over your garment. Air needs to flow freely through leather.

17) *Linen:* Linen often has a very textured, gauzy look. Its light, semi-sheer quality convinces many people in hot locations to wear this filmy material. While the "Cuban drug lord" look is very sexy on the right man, a Dirty Diva can also look smoldering in linen. Wearing it can really bring attention to your attributes (tits).

How did furniture polish get on my pretty linen shirt? Jose pinned me against his freshly polished mahogany coffee table, and he used my back to buff away the excess cleaner. I have to say, I really didn't care about my shirt at the time.

MATERIALS

If you need to remove a stain from a linen item, hopefully you've had a night of hot Latin love to show for it. If not, have some, and then consult this section again.

Circulate the garment through the warm-water cycle using a mild detergent. Dry it slightly by machine, and then iron it. Generally, the heavier the fabric, the hotter the iron should be.

18) ***Metal:*** Yes, I've found a way to get spew in my earrings. I decided not to let Elliot ravage me on my lunchbreak. Instead, I let him bust a nut in my hair (I was feeling particularly virtuous at the time). His cock snot was so plentiful that not only did he soak my hair but he saturated my earrings too. If you've ever had this happen, you're a good little Dirty Diva. If not, you and your lover are long overdue for a trip to Tiffany & Co. to obtain some jewelry to defile. To make your outing to the store extra pleasurable, make sure to alert your rug fluffer that you neglected to wear any underwear.

For precious metals other than silver, you may soak the metal in equal parts warm water and baking soda for about 10 minutes and then clean gently with a baby's toothbrush or soft cloth. Finally, rinse with water and dry gently with an absorbent towel. You may use your sugar daddy's denture tablets in lieu of baking soda, but be sure to use the proportions as directed on the package.

Silver is unique in that it will tarnish more than any other metal. Because of this, it needs to be treated differently. For cleaning, silver cleaner works best, but you may substitute regular toothpaste. Rub the cleanser gently into your silver jewelry, and rinse with water. If there happen to be any puke particles present, you may gently remove them with a baby's (extra-soft) toothbrush. Finally, pat dry and rub to a shine with a soft cloth.

If you've ever polished the knob, you'll find cleaning chrome, stainless steel, or other nonprecious metal to be a breeze. Glass cleaner will do just fine. Spritz a little on a lint-free cloth and rub, rub, rub until shiny and dry. This is one cleaning technique that, if practiced regularly, will cause your grateful boyfriend to blow his load for you. Isn't that just the sweetest thing you've ever heard?

19) *Mohair (also see "Wool"):* Leave it to me to somehow get a spunk stain in my mohair sweater. I love that sweater and, fortunately, it wasn't too hard to wash that man right out of it. Now, when I wear it, I only *feel* dirty because in reality, I'm clean.

Hand wash mohair items in cold running water. Because you're working with cold water, find a detergent that easily dissolves. If you can't find this special kind of soap, you can just dissolve normal detergent in a small amount of water. If you don't use this special soap, or if you use regular laundry detergent without first dissolving it, you'll end up with too much lather or tons of detergent granules embedded in your mohair. Believe me, no girl wants granules in her mohair pie! After you're satisfied with the cleanliness of your garment, press as much of the water as you can out of the mohair with a clean towel. Finally, lay flat to dry.

MATERIALS

20) Nylon: Brought to the clothing market in the 1950s, nylon has made women's lives so much easier. We went from silk stockings that needed to be held up with garter belts to pantyhose that are easily pulled up over our booties. However, even with all of our advances, there isn't anything sexier than silk stockings held up by garter belts which, I should add, is definitely Dirty Diva style. Sometimes, the oldies are the goodies.

Peter really liked to add various foods to my plentiful bush buffet. In fact, he once managed to soak my nylons in chocolate sauce. Actually, I really didn't care what he liked to eat, as long as it involved me!

If materials could be related, nylon and acetate would be cousins. Nylon is a manmade material like plastic. Just as you wouldn't toss plastic wrap into the hot wash load, you wouldn't do so with nylon either. Follow the directions that you would for acetate.

21) Plastic: The main reason you would need to clean plastic is because you need to defunk your mechanical muff muncher. However, things like plastic bottles and tool handles are also not safe from the grips of the Dirty Diva. Keep your sex toys clean; otherwise, your beaver will swell to the size of a Sasquatch.

Make sure to unplug and/or turn off all electrical and battery-operated toys. I can't imagine anything more embarrassing than a Dirty Diva's mother coming to identify her daughter's body fried to a giant dildo (unless it's a Dirty Diva's mother coming to identify her daughter's body fried to a tiny one). Make a solution of equal parts vinegar and warm water.

Does the mixture remind you of anything? It should. Basically, it's the recipe for douche. Why mess with perfection? Use a baby's toothbrush to apply the mixture until clean. Next, use a damp towel to remove any excess vinegar mixture, and wipe with a clean, dry towel. If you're very germ conscious, apply a tiny amount of hand sanitizer to your toy. If you do this, however, make sure the sanitizer has completely vaporized before reinjecting your chubby chum.

For all other plastic items, glass cleaner is perfectly acceptable.

22) *Polyester:* I would like to give sexual favors to whoever created polyester. Ironing really brings out the diva in me. I hate to iron so much that I will actually go through the trouble of rewashing clothes to moisten them so that I can throw them into the dryer to eliminate wrinkles. Polyester wrinkles so infrequently. It's perfect for when I'm out all night, stay over a stranger's house, and need to go straight to work in the morning. Even though what I wear to work was sitting in a crumpled pile on somebody's floor earlier that morning (and if it weren't for the fact that everyone saw what I had on the day before), no one at the office would ever know I'm not wearing freshly laundered garments! Impulsiveness is sexy, and you can be very impulsive with polyester clothing. Without having to iron, you can get ready for a date or leave town at the drop of a hat, while throwing together a rich-looking outfit.

If you're like me and you've just gotten lipstick on the crotch of your married lover's polyester-blend pants, then it is

MATERIALS

imperative that you effectively attack the stain. The sanctity of a marriage is riding on your fast-acting skills!

Put polyester items in the warm-water cycle. Tumble dry low, and remove immediately. Don't tumble dry too long or you'll ruin the fabric. Ironing can be tricky because you can create those shiny marks if you use too high a setting. Make sure to use a lukewarm iron. Remember, you wouldn't iron plastic wrap with a hot iron. Plastic and polyester respond similarly to an iron; they melt.

23) *Rayon:* Rayon can be very sexy. It feels cool on a hot night. It skims the figure. It flows with the body, and it usually has a silky and filmy feel to the touch. Your lover will get all worked up with one touch of your sexy rayon garment.

During a ravaging rainstorm rendezvous, mud plastered my favorite rayon shirt. The shirt I can clean anytime, but Jason + doggie style in the backyard = priority.

Try to get as much of the offending substance off the rayon as possible. You must then take this one to your dry cleaner. For future reference, be sure to aim your guy's member somewhere else when he's letting it go.

24) *Satin (also see "Silk"):* Satin is even sexier than rayon, especially because satin is usually worn between the sheets—and sometimes it *is* the sheets. Dirty Divas know that slippery sex is best, and it's even better on slippery sheets. Be careful because if you're too fervent a lover, you'll slip-slide your ass right off the satin-dressed bed.

Treat satin the same way you would any manmade fiber. Machine wash your fabric in cold or warm water, and tumble dry on the low cycle. You may be lucky enough to have acquired a satin piece made from actual silk. The feel is so much more decadent than the cheaper manmade version. Care for this piece as you would care for silk.

25) *Silk:* Silk is ultimately the sexiest garment. It is the Rolls Royce of fabrics, the Godiva of materials. Silk is sexy not only because of its texture, but because it's produced in a very primordial way. Essentially, silk is the excretion of the silkworm. Like fur and leather, silk is harvested from a living organism. There's something intensely primal about wearing a garment made from the excretion of a phallic life-form (like that of the silk worm). Our usually restricted human senses must perceive this at some level because in silk, we effortlessly ooze sexuality. There's no other material that gives instant free bonus points like that.

If you're one to read those raunchy romance novels, you'll notice that the heroine is always adorned in flowing silk before it is ripped from her quivering bosom. Those who have the money choose to get silk sheets for their regal quality. Kings and queens have been wearing silk for thousands of years.

Silk is so sexy because it flows like rayon and satin, yet it's different in that nothing can compare to the sensation of it on bare skin. Why else would the expression "silky smooth" have come about?

It is best to dry-clean silk. Remember what I said about aiming your guy's member somewhere else when he's about to let it go on your nice rayon garment? The same goes for silk. Like satin, silk can sometimes be hand or machine washed. I have two Banana Republic silk shirts that are machine washable. Check your labels. If you're not sure about cleaning a silk garment, it's better to take it to your dry cleaner.

26) Spandex: Okay, so you're an '80s fiend. "Let's get physical ... physical ... let me hear your body talk." Apparently, spandex (well, spandex or leg warmers) is all that's required for Olivia to get physical with anyone. I'd say getting physical with *her* is definitely worth wearing spandex, but the leg warmers may be a bit of a stretch. There's no way a Dirty Diva could not be tempted to wear spandex. It hugs the body so close that it's sometimes hard to know where the spandex ends and the body begins. Wearing spandex is a veritable advertisement of what you have to offer to a potential fuck puppet because a man or woman can immediately see what it is that he or she wants to touch or lick on you. (Note: if you have cellulite or are considerably overweight, wearing spandex might actually turn off would-be lovers, so wear it cautiously.)

Now, how to get tree sap out of leggings after you've gone bird's nesting:

You can clean spandex in the cold- or warm-water cycle. If you put spandex in the dryer, take it out before it's completely dry; otherwise, you'll ruin the fabric. Spandex responds best to being naturally dried.

27) Stone: Is there anything you haven't managed to defile? Somehow you produce a sex stain on the hearth of your fireplace, yet you remain completely unapologetic! What's that you say? It wasn't you? Oh. Silly me. It must've been me! Sorry.

Cleaning concrete, stone, or pavement is easy as can be. Mix one cup of baking soda (or denture tablets as directed) with one gallon of warm water, scrub into the surface with a coarse brush, and rinse well with water. If the surface is shiny, use a soft brush, and rinse well with water.

When you've gotta have it, you've gotta have it. Ergo, for those times when your girlfriend takes you, hosting your monthly visitor, on the garage floor, you'll need to know how to clean heavier stains (like blood) off concrete. Wow, your girlfriend's very nasty, and that's very hot—almost *too* hot. But there is nothing too hot for a Dirty Diva! Anyway, mix one cup of ammonia with one gallon of warm water, scrub into the stain, and rinse with water 10 times.

Your precious stones need love too. The easiest and most thorough way to clean precious stones is to use a self-contained jewelry cleaner that you would commonly find in commercial jewelry stores. Otherwise, mix two tablespoons of baking soda with one cup of water, gently brush the mixture onto the stone with a baby's toothbrush, and rinse with the coldest water possible (rinsing with hot water makes stones misty, while cold water makes them fog free). Buff to a high shine with a soft cloth.

28) *Suede:* Remember my introduction? Vomit on my gorgeous Jones New York stilettos? They're suede, and it was heartbreaking. I was using vodka tonics to drown away the memory of a certain little lawyer when my stomach decided it had had enough. In retrospect, it's probably better that it didn't work out with the lawyer— he had hair plugs and an unusually drippy dick. I've never seen anything like it in my Dirty Diva life. Either my very presence launched him into a perpetual orgasm or he was always trying to water his houseplants without ever getting off his bed. At least the Ralph Lauren sheets that he showered in his man juice were *his*. Although I was temporarily heartbroken over Drippy Dick, all was not lost when I was able to restore my shoes to their natural beauty. All better!

For suede, you may safely apply a little vinegar to the stain and allow it to dry. Follow with gentle strokes using a suede brush.

Most professionals tell you not to do what I'm about to tell you, but it worked fine for me. If you're not comfortable taking the chance on your suede item, take it to the cleaners. If you have a daring spirit, however, barely moisten an abrasive plastic (no steel wool) sponge, and work the material with tender, deliberate strokes going in one direction. Do not rub in a vigorous back-and-forth motion. This will cause the suede to deteriorate. The aforementioned directions also apply to pleasing your girlfriend in a stranger's bedroom at a party. Of course, you'll have to substitute your finger for the abrasive sponge.

29) *Velour/Velvet:* Velvet is a very luxurious fabric that arouses daydreams of sophisticated men and women lounging at European villas overlooking the sea. I picture them wearing plush velvet robes, lying beside a sapphire blue swimming pool. Of course, my daydream always ends with the man and the woman naked in the pool. They're able to get into astounding positions because of their buoyancy in the water. Naturally, the 18-year-old houseboy enters, and after he joins them, the three enlist the help of the butler's daughter. First, the two sophisticates are enjoying some one-on-one action, while the wide-eyed youths savor each other. Then, there comes the exciting swinging action. The older man with the younger woman, and the older woman with the younger man ... Ooh ... oh, God ... I'm on my way! Almost there... whoops, sorry. I didn't mean to do that to you again!

Let's get back on track. After all is done, how can the sophisticates possibly clean their exquisite velvet garments?

They need to have the houseboy take them to the dry cleaners. He should not attempt to clean the velvet himself. In the future, however, should the velvet fibers appear worn, he can spritz a bit of water on the fabric and brush the fibers with a lint brush (not roller) to fluff.

30) *Wood:* I am not talking about a stiffy—I'm talking about the table you need to clean after your hasty 10-minute liaison with Speed Racer. As with glass, there is more than one reason you'll need to clean wood. First, you'll need to clean stains or substances off the wood. You'll also need to remove surface scratches. (I see you still haven't trimmed your funky-ass nails.)

MATERIALS

The superficial cleaning of wood is the easiest. Apply a little furniture polish to a soft, clean cloth, and glide it over your wood furniture. If you can't find any furniture polish, spray a tiny amount of cooking spray on the cloth instead.

For disguising fine scratches on wood furniture, use color-matching wood filler or a color-matching children's crayon to fill ridges. Follow the directions specified on the package for the wood filler. If you choose to use the children's crayon, slightly heat it with a lighter, rub it into the ridge, and wipe away any excess with a dry, lint-free cloth.

31) *Wool:* Can wool be sexy? Sometimes.

Sexy is a woman in a wool skirt and riding boots. What she is about to ride is her little secret. Sexier is a woman in a wool skirt, riding boots, and holding a leather whip. A woman can also exude sexiness in a cozy wool sweater with a good-fitting pair of jeans. But, generally, wool is not sexy. Wool can also trap some nasty odors, so make sure you launder your woolen garments at least every other time you wear them.

For cleaning instructions, follow the steps under "Mohair."

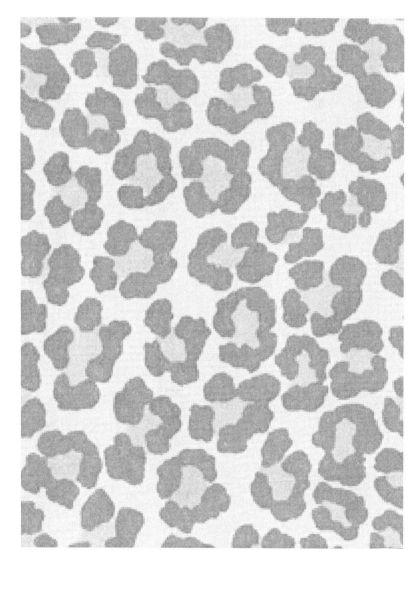

5

SEX-INDUCED STAINS

*T*HESE ARE THE MOST common stains. I've had good luck with the cleaning techniques I'm about to reveal to you. However, all materials and fabrics respond differently. For your own protection, follow the manufacturer's cleaning directions first. **Again, it's important that you first adhere to the directions on garment labels before following any advice in the section below.**

*1) **Antiperspirant/Deodorant:*** When I'm sweatin' with an oldie, I don't like it to show on my clothes. An older man is better in bed because he's more grateful to be with a young, attractive woman than is a younger man. My statement has resulted in much contention, most of which comes from younger men who have been systematically unable to prove me wrong. They'll contend that because they're younger, they have more energy or stamina, but when push comes to shove, all that energy and stamina is mainly concentrated on themselves. Their energy must have been self-concentrated because it sure as hell wasn't for my benefit! I can't say that I don't often enjoy my interactions with these greenhorns who try to refute my belief, but in the end, their efforts are all in vain.

Antiperspirant stains are a bitch to clean. The perfect mix of oils and aluminum chloride is what helps keep us sweat free. Unfortunately, that same sweat-seeking mixture also clings to fabric, attracting body oils and creating yellow stains.

You must attack the antiperspirant stain with rubbing alcohol and then launder in the hottest possible water. Some people claim vinegar will work in lieu of alcohol, but I find that the alcohol performs better, unlike my younger counterparts in bed.

*2) **Body fluids:***

 *a) **Blood:*** Blood can arrive on the scene in several different ways.

 First, you or your girlfriend gets her period. This starts the explosion of horny outbursts, and before you know it, there are marks left all around the house, as if a critical teacher were tearing through the place with a big red magic marker.

Second, it could get so crazy that you or your lover actually draws blood. If so, congratulations! You deserve the Dirty Diva distinction! I never condone any kind of non-consensual behavior, but if you and your vampire partner enjoy tasting *all* of each other, then more power to you! The attraction for blood in sex can be so deep-seated in a person's psyche that he/she may actually not be able to cum without the taste of blood. When I was eleven, I was friends with an oversexed girl who believed that she was a bona fide vampire. There's no doubt in my mind that blood plays an integral part in her sex life today.

Finally, there may come a time when you need to clean large amounts of blood out of your car trunk. I've never heard of a product called "Homicide Hide," but in its absence, there are some cleansers that you can use to banish the stubborn bloodstain.

For our first and second scenarios, the following technique is very effective for eliminating any offensive red spots. Blood contains proteins that need to be broken down at the core, and meat tenderizer is the best combatant. Make a thick mixture of tenderizer and water, and apply to wherever you or your girlfriend may have spotted. Allow the mixture to work on the stain for 30 to 45 minutes, and then rinse well with water.

Promptly take dry-clean-only items to the cleaners to avoid lingering brown spots from set-in bloodstains. Adding a little cold water and salt to a bloody spot on a dry-clean-only garment could ward off the stain until you get to the cleaners, so try it.

Our final scenario depicts you needing to eliminate massive amounts of blood from the trunk of your car. If you ever find yourself in that situation, stay the hell away from me, and call Mark Geragos immediately.

Special note for blood on leather: You got blood on Nick's leather car interior when you savagely pushed him into his backseat and demanded a bawdy boning. Apparently, his Mont Blanc was lying on the seat harmlessly, until it got lodged in his ass cheek. If it's happened once, it's happened a thousand times. Apply a small amount of 3% hydrogen peroxide (the kind you use to clean blood off yourself) to the stained leather, and allow it to bubble. Clean with a damp cloth, and dry.

b) Fecal matter: Let's get anal, people! There are different strokes for different folks. If you enjoy scatting, chances are before heading to the bedroom, you and your date go to the all-you-can-eat buffet to ensure that you are both armed with plenty of cocoa-colored ammo.

Although the following story is not directly related to a sexual act, I really feel that the Dirty Diva inside you will appreciate its spirit. As long as I live, I'll never forget an incident that occurred when I brought a particular guy, whom I'll refer to as Brownstar, to a friend's party. My gracious friend allowed us to sleep over at her house along with about 20 other people. After a wild night of drinking and heavy petting, the guy and I woke up the next morning in the middle of my friend's floor with about 10 others. In the middle of a conversation, Brownstar stood up to reveal that he was in his undershirt and tighty whities (everyone else was fully clothed). He then headed for the bathroom. As I was checking out his ass, I suddenly noticed that he had a tennis-ball-size brown spot on the back of his underwear. Performing a double take, I remained calm so as not to draw attention to Brownstar's predicament. The crowd dispersed before he returned to the room. Thankfully, I never had to contend with any snide comments from the others. I found out that he was really heavy into cocaine, and he had been doing a lot of it the night before. I never mentioned to Brownstar that he had fudged his cupcakes that day, but I don't lose sleep over it. Since finding out he was a major cokehead, I'm pretty sure he wouldn't care if I told him about his complete loss of bowel control.

Whether intentional or accidental, squirting chocolate syrup around in the bedroom brings the likelihood of stubborn stains to clean.

Scrape as much of the feces off the sheets as possible. Then, soak in very cold water, apply laundry soap to the stain, wash briskly, and rinse in fresh cold water. If there's a pesky brown stain still remaining after washing, apply a mixture of equal parts cold water and rubbing alcohol to the stain, and wash again.

c) *Perspiration (including sweat stains, handprints, and footprints):* Preceding vigorous vaginal exercise, working up a sweat is usually required. When you perspire, you unwittingly transmit your scent to a would-be lover. He smells your scent and the nerve impulses in his nose then send a message to the limbic system in his brain. There, it's determined whether he wants to bone you. If your aroma pleases his brain chemistry, then you get laid! If his chemistry is not approving of your scent, he'll walk right past you.

I used to be really uptight about the thought that a man might be able to smell my special body scent during sex. I was so uptight that I spent useless energy worrying and trying to mask my true Dirty Diva scent with perfumes, deodorants, and lotions. But after a little education on the subject of sexual chemistry, my apprehensions diminished. I finally realized that smelling *only* perfume or deodorant on someone's body is not much of a turn-on. However, being able to detect someone's raw, unadulterated scent is extremely sexy. I also realized that as a result of following my nose, I had found myself immensely sexually attracted to some rather physically unattractive individuals. In fact, I've felt compelled to sleep with a certain grotesque brown-bagger because his mouth-watering scent was more than I could resist. These realizations helped me overcome some of my self-image anxieties.

When you finally merge with someone whose scent makes you wild with desire, you will usually experience an intense feeling that you know him more intimately (even if he is just another one-night stand). Others may try to conceal their true identity with cologne.

Please do not interpret any of this to mean that you should not wear *any* perfume or deodorant. Also, for God's sake, don't neglect to shave your damn pits!

It's so easy to clean perspiration stains. Launder clothes as normal. Any remaining stains will an amalgamation of sweat with another substance such as antiperspirant or deodorant (see "Antiperspirant").

Foot and handprints on car windows are easily wiped away with a dry cloth and glass cleaner. Use old-fashioned furniture polish from an aerosol can for prints on wooden tables.

d) *Semen/Feminine moisture:* Ahh, the pinnacle of all sex stains: the cream of the cock—the honey from the pot. This specific stain even inspired this book. Although I once found semen stains disgusting and dirty, I now regard them as trophies of my sexual prowess. Only you and a certain White House intern must know how I feel about this subject. Indeed, *I* would never keep my trophy for an extended period of time, but I can understand the desire to do so.

When I spot a sex stain on any of my belongings, I suddenly remember the power I had at one moment in time to bring a man to uncontrollable heights of pleasure. When the time finally comes that you must eradicate a love squirt, however, make sure you know what you're doing.

Different men produce different sperm. The same goes for women and their moisture. Thankfully, there's one way to clean all that anyone produces. When dry, scrape off as much of the raised substance as possible. Then, make a mixture of plain (unseasoned) meat tenderizer and water, and apply it to the scraped area. Plain meat tenderizer is made up of special enzymes that naturally decompose protein fibers, which makes it the perfect clean-up solution for Ian's ultimate protein shake. After allowing the mixture to permeate the stain for about 30 to 45 minutes, you can clean your clothes as you normally would or take them to the cleaners without any cause for shame. Now, don't you feel like you've unlocked the secrets to the universe?

e) ***Urine:*** "I'm singin' in the rain! I'm singin' in the rain!" Did I mention the rain was yellow? Golden showers, anyone? Does your lover like you to cop a squat over his chest, or do you prefer to be showered in the warm amber droplets? Often, what's strange to you is sexually exciting to someone else. (Personally, I like getting my hair pulled and sometimes enjoy a slightly restricted air supply.) To further illustrate my point, I have to tell you that my ex-boyfriend with

SEX-INDUCED STAINS

the foot fetish once got very vocal about how "disgusting" yellow showers are. Hellooo? Does he not realize that the mere idea of a sockless foot (not to mention toes wriggling around inside a salivating mouth) is enough to force some people (including one of my best friends) into a 10-minute dry-heave spell? Guess not.

Keith enjoyed having you relieve yourself on his thigh. Now you need to remove the unsightly stain from your mattress pad. Not only do you want to eradicate the stain, but you probably also want to do away with the smell.

Soak a piss stain right away in ice-cold water for five minutes. Then, using liquid laundry detergent (or equal parts rubbing alcohol and cold water), apply a small amount to the spot and allow it to penetrate for another five minutes. Finally, launder as you normally would. After cleansing the area, lightly dust with baking soda to absorb any lingering odors. Some professionals recommend using ammonia in lieu of liquid laundry detergent, but the scent of ammonia is reminiscent of the smell of urine. In my opinion, trying to rid a urine stain/smell with something that smells just like urine is counterproductive.

f) ***Vomit:*** Who hasn't gotten fucked up on Mad Dog 20/20 and run naked with her friends through the suburban streets of Baltimore? Oh, just me? I can't be the *only* one to have gotten wasted and found myself sitting in a public bathroom sink crying over some guy. If you've never gotten drunk, puked all over yourself or someone else, and then slept with someone you shouldn't have, you are not a true Dirty Diva. I urge you (if you are 21 years of age or older) to go to your local liquor store, pick up a bottle of Manischewitz and drink its entire contents. Next, proceed to your nearest neighborhood bar (in a cab, of course), and behave accordingly. The morning after your crazed outing, call the cab to pick your ass up from that strange house, come home, shower, and resume reading this section.

The very act of cleaning vomit can induce vomiting. Before attempting to wash any item free of a vomit stain, dab a little scented oil below your nose to mask the smell of the offending substance. Next, scrape away as much of the chunky matter as you can. Then, immerse the stained area in cold water for 10 to 15 minutes. If there are still chunks remaining, you can turn the fabric over and allow a strong, steady stream of cold water to push out any lingering particles. Now, apply liquid laundry detergent (or equal parts rubbing alcohol and cold water) to the stain and let it stand for five to 10 minutes. Launder as usual.

3) *Burn marks:* Ooh, baby, c'mon and light my fire. Wait. Hey, stop. Stop it! I said "Light my fire," not "Burn the crap out of my tits with your father's Zippo!"

When I see a physically attractive man, I often refer to him as "hot." I've also often designated my love affairs as "steamy," "sizzling," and "scorching"—all denoting heat. Of course, I'm not suggesting that the attractive man and my affairs are literally hot. I'm speaking metaphorically. Some

Dirty Divas, however, delight in taking a hot and steamy love affair to the literal level.

For some of us, getting burned is sexually gratifying. Building bonfires and watching houses burn to the ground is very exciting to a pyromaniac, but burning for sexual satisfaction (pyrophilia) is an entirely different thrill. Just as you may go crazy when someone rubs your ass, sucks your ears, or scratches your back, the pyrophiliac reaches her potent climax through skin singeing. The feeling she experiences going from zero to 60 in about a second is exciting and frightening at the same time. It's exciting for her because each scorching singe causes her heart rate to soar. Of course, when the heat source is removed, her heart rate will slow down. Once the heat contacts her skin again, her heart rate goes back up. Soar ... plummet. Soar ... plummet. Those ups and downs are what cause the pyrophiliac to burn for sexual pleasure. Getting burned can also be somewhat frightening because the "burnee" never knows when or where to expect the next sear. Therefore, each partner has to trust the other to the highest degree.

If you and Simon have ruined your favorite blouse by "heating things up," you can fight fire with fire. Leave the garment to dry naturally in the sun after immediately immersing the seared area in cold water.

If that doesn't work, try to cool things down a bit. Again, immerse the seared area in cold water, but apply a little bleach (for white garments), and launder as usual. You will probably need to repeat the process several times because once a garment is burned, it will be very difficult to remove the discoloration. While stains change the color of the fabric, burns change the very integrity of the material. So have patience, and try to remember to remove your clothes before you get down in the disco inferno.

4) *Food/Drink:*

a) Alcoholic beverages (also see "Wine"): Dirty Divas wouldn't be nearly as dirty as they are without alcohol. Let's have a moment of silence to pay homage to the DD's preferred beverage.

If a woman walks into a bar and orders a glass of wine, she is deemed classy and sophisticated. If the same woman had ordered a scotch on the rocks, probably every man in that bar would have turned his head because scotch isn't considered a "ladylike" drink. Nothing says "dirty" like a woman walking into a bar and ordering hard liquor. Of course, we DDs do tend to be unconventional.

You walk into the bar and order your hard liquor like a pro. While placing your order, you catch the eye of a very impressed and handsome man named Adam. Being the fuckaholics you are, you both decide to take the party back

SEX-INDUCED STAINS

to his place. You follow him through an extremely upscale neighborhood and down a long, winding driveway. As you pull up next to his car, you notice there's another already sitting in the driveway. You both enter through the kitchen to see a beautiful woman washing dishes. At that time, he informs you that the woman is his wife, Sandra, and that he thought you would enjoy getting to know her. You're not into the idea at first, but Sandra graciously opens her home to you and offers you a drink. You decide that this could be a lot of fun. Adam leaves the room and returns a short time later, producing a bottle of Remy Martin. He requests that you be Sandra's glass. You happily oblige.

As you drive home the next morning, you are reminded of Adam and Sandra by an aching in your crotch. Later, you're reminded of them again when you catch a glimpse of your clothes. Immediately soak any alcohol stains in cold water or club soda. Then, apply a mixture of equal parts water and liquid laundry detergent to the stain. Rinse well with cold water.

If you've been keeping company with not-so-well-to-do swingers, you'll probably find that your clothes are covered in beer. Mix equal parts vinegar and water, and apply to the stain. Rinse well with cool water.

To keep your dry-clean-only items stain free until you get to the cleaners, thoroughly dab water on the offending spots.

b) Butter/Margarine: Mmmm—buttered buns—my favorite! Mmmm—Jude's buttered buns—even better! Have you ever brought food lube into your boudoir? I have, and boy, did I get one hell of a surprise on my carpet. You'd think that because butter is so light in color that it wouldn't stain light-colored carpet. Wrong! The oils from butter wreak havoc on any type of material, causing you tremendous aggravation trying to get it out. The only good part about that butter stain on the carpet was that the Mohawk between my legs got just as messy as the one on the floor (Stainguard, my ass).

If you'd like to rid a butter/margarine stain from one of your sexy garments, scrape off as much of the excess as possible with the side of a fork or a butter knife. Next, apply a little liquid dishwashing soap to the stain and allow it to rest for five to 10 minutes. At first, that may not make sense, but think back to all the dishwashing liquid commercials you've seen. Notice how they all boast "grease-cutting capabilities"? They actually do what they claim, so there's no reason you can't utilize those means to launder. Finally, rinse in cool to lukewarm water, and dry.

For cleaning the Mohawk on the floor, sprinkle baking soda or cornstarch into the stain, and massage. Allow the baking soda to absorb all the oil by waiting 45 minutes. Finally, vacuum up the baking soda.

c) ***Chocolate/Chocolate syrup:*** No one believes that I don't go a day without eating some type of chocolate. My friends say that I like my chocolate like I like my men: strong, rich, and ample. There's something to this aphrodisiac that keeps me coming back for more. Naturally, the Dirty Diva loves the ultimate aphrodisiacal food, and it's not something as mundane as licorice. Have you ever wondered why you feel like you could give up sex forever in exchange for just one bite of the sweet stuff? The reason is that chocolate contains elements that deliver messages to the pleasure part of the brain, including the good old limbic system, which gives you a very satisfied feeling. That's probably why when I'm feeling especially horny with no men in sight, I reach for a Hershey's chocolate bar. Sometimes, even if there are *plenty* of men in sight, I still reach for the Hershey's!

The merging of sex and chocolate is an especially hedonistic union. While sex is undeniably carnal, chocolate is downright self-indulgent (because there's really no nutritional value to speak of). Carnal self-indulgence = hedonism. Because chocolate has such an erotic effect, bringing it into the bedroom seems like a very natural transition for me.

Bryan and I once made use of an entire bottle of chocolate syrup during one ravenous encounter. Everything, including my hair, sheets, carpet, and his pants, was affected. While he was licking the sticky, delicious substance from my left lip, I looked around my room and decided I would need to get all new linens and clothes. After he moved to my right lip, I thought, "I could really give a shit about my goddamn sheets right now," and I began to concentrate on my delightful tongue-lashing.

Are you all hot and bothered now? I'll bet you're dying to know what any Dirty Diva in your position would want to know: "How did she end up cleaning all that mess?" Am I right?

For a chocolate stain, apply a little ammonia to the discolored area, and launder as usual. If, however, the stain is very fresh, you may soak the discolored area in club soda or equal parts water and liquid laundry detergent for 10 to 15 minutes. After soaking, launder as usual.

d) Fruit/Fruit juice (also see "Wine"): Voraciously ripping at the flesh of a succulent fresh peach with your teeth is pretty damn sexy. Sexier is when the juice from the fruit drips down your chin into your cleavage. Sexiest is when the juice is deliberately licked from your majestic mounds by a hot chick.

Mentally take note of how a man or a woman consumes juicy pieces of fruit. It's commonly felt that the way a person eats his/her fruit is indicative of how well he/she will give head. If the person in question timidly nibbles at a fresh, juicy plum, then chances are that person won't give it his/her all when going down on you. On the other hand, if he/she ravenously tears into the plum, then you've hit the cunnilingus jackpot.

My accountant is coming to my house to do my income taxes tomorrow. He'll set up his computer at my kitchen table and get down to business. Innocently enough, I'll offer him a nice piece of fruit. In between his bites, he'll be talking about deductions and liabilities, but I'll be thinking about something else. He's a married man, but I can dream, can't I?

Have you ever enthusiastically fed your lover grapes in bed? If you have, then you've probably found the tiny orbs squished into your favorite nightgown afterwards. The best way to remove the stain is to douse it in cold water and rub liquid laundry detergent rigorously into the stain. Then, run it under hot water to remove. If the stain remains, pour a little baking soda on the stain, rub, and follow with hot water. Finally, launder as usual. After you've removed the stain, go back to bed, and give your man something else to eat.

*e) **Gum:*** Have you ever caught a whiff of your rancid breath while you and your date were en route to a fancy restaurant? If so, what would you do? You'd pop a piece of gum in your mouth, of course.

I always chew gum before a date or a fuck. I feel like that minty little stick gives me the guarantee of fresh breath even if I chewed the fish right before my date arrived. When you're on the dating scene, a reputation for having bad breath is the kiss of death. The only thing worse is being reputed to have morning pussy! If you could care less, good for you! You are a true Dirty Diva because you realize that you are sexy and you are human, which does not require you to be perfect all the time. Unfortunately, some of us are a little self-conscious and need the artificial help. Chewing gum may rescue you from bad breath, but it also leaves you vulnerable to other dangers.

In his parents' bed, Jimmy was devouring your hair pie while you were chomping away on some gum. Really, it's not that sick—his parents were away on vacation in Venice. Just as the spitting from your grassed geyser erupted, you released a moan and your gum accidentally fell from your mouth. Although your gum became lodged securely in his parent's sheets, the bond that you and Jimmy shared was well worth the trouble of having to eliminate the mess. Now, you'll still need to clean the propelled wad (are we still talking about gum?) out of the sheets to prevent his parents from growing hip to the jaunt on their bed. One other thing—they're due back tomorrow. Damn, you're always stuck in these tight spots.

Scrape off as much of the gooey stuff up as you can with a dull edge, perhaps a butter knife. Then, place a piece of brown paper over the gum stain. Finally, let's get *hot*, baby. Iron until the gum sticks to the paper entirely. If there is still gum remaining, apply a small amount of peanut butter to the stain, allow it to rest for five to 10 minutes, and peel away. Of course, once you bring out the peanut butter, you and Jimmy may not be able to resist another bender. I just love peanut butter on a log!

If the aforesaid cleaning technique does not work, find out where Jimmy's parents got their sheets and do the old "switcheroo."

f) ***Ice cream:*** I scream, you scream, we all scream for slice-cream! Incidentally, slice cream is best when served on a glazed doughnut.

If you've ever brought ice cubes along for your Randy ride, you know how stimulating cold stuff can be. Nothing brings my guns' bullets to attention quite like ice cream and Randy. Ice is sexy because it sends shivers down the spine of the one getting "iced." Ice cream is sexier, however, not only because it sends shivers down the spine of the "iced" person but also because its delicious taste begs to be licked off a body. First, you experience the scintillating physical reaction to the extreme freeze, which sends goose bumps all over your body. Then, there is the immediate contrasting thaw of a warm mouth. Similar to pyrophilia, ice play also presents the electrifying and frightening elements. The electric element is represented by the intense physical reaction to the freezing cold. Not knowing what is going to happen or when it's going to happen represents the fright element. Of course, it can also be pretty frightening when Randy spoons ice cream onto your pants instead of your pie, which he was about to eat a la mode. How do you handle it?

Usually, all can be removed with a little club soda and some old-fashioned elbow grease. A mixture of equal parts plain meat tenderizer and water may also be applied to the stain. Allow the mixture to penetrate for 45 minutes, and then rinse with cold water. Whichever method you implement, follow by laundering as usual.

*g) **Jell-O:*** Considering it is just food, Jell-O is oddly reminiscent of the female form. It wiggles and jiggles just like a real woman. Who hasn't dreamt of women wrestling in the squishy stuff? I have, and I am a woman. Jell-O is also sweet, which makes it the perfect treat to garnish those sometimes not-so-sweet body parts during sexual activities. It's especially delicious when being slurped off a sexy person's belly button.

If you haven't yet had the opportunity to do so, you should host a party at which you provide Jell-O shots. Make the shots extra strong so that everyone gets sufficiently drunk. Before you know it, you'll have plenty of chances to swallow shots from sexy, quaking body parts. Of course, in order to slurp Jell-O from a *sexy* person's belly button, you'll actually need to invite sexy people. A body shot just isn't sexy when it's slurped off a flabby stomach; it must be sucked off a hot bod. Make sure your party's itinerary is as accommodating to the "beautiful people" as possible to ensure that your soiree is the sexiest it can be.

Basically, Jell-O consists of water and dye (and a little bit of gelatin). Treat a Jell-O stain the same as you would a dye stain. Always douse the stain in cold water immediately. Then, after getting your jollies, pull the fabric taut, and allow it to sit under cold running water as long as you can stand (up to eight hours). Pull yourself away from your fuck buddy long enough to be sure that the water is not overflowing. It's plenty effective if the flow is slow and steady; it doesn't need to be gushing. If there are any discolorations remaining, try a little vinegar directly on the stain. Allow the vinegar to penetrate for five to 10 minutes, and rinse in cold water. Launder as usual.

*h) **Mayonnaise:*** You step up to the fast food counter and ask, "May I have the deluxe with the mayo on the side?" I say, "Forget putting the mayo on the side! On the contrary, slather it on your fuzzburger as thick as you like without any worries of elevating your cholesterol levels."

Does mayo remind you of anything? It should. Mayonnaise is suspiciously similar to both pecker and flap snot. If you're a Dirty Diva, you can't look at a jar of

Miracle Whip without getting all juiced up. This is one condiment that won't prevent a pregnancy because it may induce one.

Mayo is a great man lube because it contains 50 percent oil. Although it is not suggested as an internal lube for womankind, Dennis is not prohibited from sucking it off your external body parts. So go ahead and allow your hottie to enjoy a little creamy mixture on your meat—you'll both come out winners.

To get mayo off your valuables, follow the cleaning directions in the "Oil/Grease" section.

i) **Mustard:** Who doesn't love mustard on a thick, juicy hot dog? Perhaps you don't go for hot dogs and you prefer mustard on top of a hearty meat pie. Whatever a girl prefers, she loves to eat the cooking but hates to clean up afterwards—especially if she has to remove a mustard stain from her beloved attire. What gives mustard its beautiful, vibrant color also stains the hell out of your clothes. Because it contains a natural yellow dye called turmeric, mustard produces a very unyielding stain. When the dye from your food (see "Jell-O" section) comes in contact with your clothes, it clings to the fibers and doesn't let go. Dye in products + contact with material = dyed material. So, hopefully, you were wearing black when the boggled bare-ass barbecue incident occurred. If not, expect that the stain will be incredibly difficult to eliminate.

Your best bet is to immediately scrape off as much excess mustard as you can. Then, douse the stain in cold water to prep for stain removal. Apply hydrogen peroxide or baking soda directly to the stain, and allow it to rest somewhere cool for 45 minutes. Finally, douse again with cold water. If the stain remains, repeat with another application of hydrogen peroxide or baking soda. Once the stain is removed, you may launder as usual.

j) ***Oil/Grease (including cooking and suntan):*** When you're out of KY, what do you do? What *do* you do? If you're like some other Dirty Divas, you open your kitchen cabinet to reveal a bountiful buffet of sexual supports. A little squirt of Pam can provide lubrication benefits comparable to the personal lubricants found in the feminine hygiene aisle. Whether you want to get out of a jam or desperately want to get into one, cooking oil and grease often serve as adequate lube (in place of your own natural moisture).

If you're opposed to looking in your kitchen cabinet for unconventional lubes, you may be inclined to use suntan oil. The pool and the shore are very sexy settings for scintillating encounters (probably because everyone is half-naked). While it's not socially acceptable to go into a bookstore and ask a patron for a massage, at places like the pool or the beach, it's perfectly okay to hand a bottle of suntan oil to a stranger and request a rubdown.

So, you're the almighty pool queen? You bestow unto the hot guy next to you your suntan oil and issue an edict ordering him to commence massaging your back immediately. Fortunately, he acknowledges your ultimate supremacy and starts on his task pronto. Despite his obedient attitude, he is not very conscientious about his duty; he continually allows his fingers to haphazardly slip under your top and into your bikini bottoms. Who are we kidding? You *love* a careless man! Oh, my, you are such a Dirty Diva. You decide to take this back to the clubhouse—there are children present, for heaven's sake!

Naturally, nothing that is touched by oil and grease stays pristine (my cousin's favorite word). There are several types of oil and grease: natural (including animal and vegetable) and manmade (automotive, not deriving from the hot delivery guy). Whatever the origin of the oil/grease stain, you can take care of it in the same ways. First, remove as much of the excess as possible by daubing with an absorbent towel. Next, sprinkle some baking soda or cornstarch evenly over the greasy stain, and allow it to rest for 20 minutes. Finally, brush off the baking soda. You may repeat this process should any grease remain. Launder as usual. If you still can't draw out the stain, dishwashing liquid will come to the rescue again! Just as it magically dissolves grease from pots and pans, liquid dishwashing detergent (LDD) will rid your pants' crotch of the stuff. Apply the LDD, and rub into a lather. Allow it to penetrate for five minutes, rinse, and launder as usual.

k) **Syrup:** Picture this: a cold winter morning, snow on the ground, a log cabin in the distance, pancakes on the griddle, maple syrup on the table. Are you hungry? Well, I'm horny. Am I the only who gets juiced up thinking of pancakes? If I catch a waft of maple syrup in the air, I think of sweet things, like the sugar stick and the honey pot. Then, I am invariably reminded of a Def Leppard song proclaiming, "I'm hot—sticky sweet, from my head to my feet. Yeah!" It's such a sexy song, full of innuendo.

Sex is often associated with sweet foods. Sometimes you may even hear someone say that the sweet treat she is eating is "better than sex." Sex and sweet foods are often associated with one another because they're both components of a decadent lifestyle, and people who lead decadent lives are always thought of as sexy. Have you ever been attracted to someone who was not in the least bit *physically* attractive? Certainly you have, and it was probably because he was either an appreciator or a spender (or he had a great scent—see "Perspiration" section), but both are equally self-indulgent. If he were the appreciative type, you would have noticed that he savored his wine a little longer than others at the table or that he basked in the sun a few more minutes than most. The spending type would have bought that Ferrari, and he certainly would have sprung for caviar instead of tuna in his lunchbox. Either of these men would view the world as his oyster. He would also seem to experience things more intensely. It's almost as if, subconsciously, the hedonist knows that his life could be over in a snap, and he may as well enjoy it while he can—"it" meaning food, nature, surroundings, or, most important to this book, sex.

If sex and sweet foods are both components of a decadent lifestyle, then it's only natural that humans would want to combine indulgences. We think, "Wow, if sex is great and syrup is great, how great would it be to combine them?"

Now that you know why someone may want to candy his/her body parts, you may need to know how to clean syrup out of mosquito netting—not that I would have any cause to know about that. But, if ever *you* have accidentally squirted the sweet stuff right past Lauren's body and into the mesh netting behind your bed, then I can only guess that you should dissolve the syrup stain by rubbing some club soda into it. Usually, this works very well because the intensely carbonated soda breaks down the sugars in the syrup—but, of course, I'm only supposing.

*l) **Tomato (including ketchup, barbeque sauce, and spaghetti sauce):*** Have some spaghetti-a! Are you Italian-a? No-a? That doesn't mean-a that you can't enjoy a little sauce on the noodle-a!

Americans aren't the only ones who like to take advantage of innocent pieces of pie. Most ethnic groups such as Italians, Greeks, and Jews are all similar in that they are passionate about food and sex. Whenever people have an equally strong passion for two things, it's only natural that they would want to bring those things together into one messy, delicious heap, which is probably why you're reading this section.

Your Italian stallion has you over for dinner. You and he decide you want to play hide-and-seek. He suggests that he hide his salami, and you think that's a scrumptious idea. The next thing you know, you're both rolling around on the delicious tomato-infused food that was intended to be your romantic dinner. Mmm, sustenance!

How does a Dirty Diva get red sauce out of an Armani jacket? First, plunge the stain into cold water (you want to get water on the front and back of the fabric). Using either vinegar or hydrogen peroxide and a baby's toothbrush, scrub the stain from the front and back of the material. Rinse well with cold water, and repeat as needed. Launder as usual.

m) ***Whipped cream:*** *Everyone* looks at a bottle of whipped cream and thinks "Fun!" Remember when you used to have whipped cream fights as a kid? Who could resist such temptation?

More than any other food, whipped cream is commonly associated with sex-play. There are several reasons for this. Number one, it's sweet (see "Syrup" section).

Second, it's a topping. Because private parts are considered by most to be sweet treats, naturally, whipped cream would be the best indulgent dessert topping for those sweet parts. Like franks to beans, whipped cream is positively the best culinary compliment to a body.

Finally, unlike any other sex food, whipped cream provides a great delivery with its ease of dispensing and its sinful sound, making for an irresistible pleasure provider. Whipped cream's packaging allows for an easy, precise application so you won't have to worry about messy leaks or spills. With the push of a nozzle, you have an instant, controllable treat. What could be easier? The sound of squirting whipped cream is especially erotic because it reminds us of the squirting from down under. When you've been blindfolded and hogtied, unable to move, you know you can be assured a good time is approaching as soon as you hear the squirting can. If, on the other hand, you hear the sound of a revving chain saw, then you know that the good times are over.

Unless Natasha is completely inept with the easy-to-use whipped cream bottle, you won't need to know how to clean the creamy stuff. However, if you are the unfortunate victim of a whipped cream whammy, follow the cleaning directions in the "Ice cream" section.

n) Wine (red): What's a Dirty Diva's favorite wine? "But I *wanna* do it again!" Wine is a necessary DD tool for three reasons. First, wine (in the right glass) is a very useful device for achieving a sophisticated image. Drinking the same drink that the sexiest people in history, including Cleopatra and Adonis, have enjoyed gives even the lowliest wench an air of sophistication. Even those who have the propensity to attend monster truck rallies will be instantly catapulted into the next highest class when seen simply holding a glass of the stuff.

Second, wine is considered the ambrosia of the gods because of the immediate knowledge one seems to get from consuming it. The fruit of the vine—ring any bells? Adam and Eve in the garden with the tree? Of course, you recall the story about humankind plucking the forbidden apple from the tree of knowledge. If you're familiar with the story, then you should remember that once the fruit was eaten, the knowledge of the world was unleashed. The same message is subconsciously applied to wine in modern times. It's as though with one sip of the fruit of the vine, the DD consumes the knowledge and experience of her ancestors. When a woman seems to be enlightened, as when she is drinking wine, she also appears sophisticated and confident. Potential lovers find enlightenment, sophistication, and confidence very alluring, so the DD tries to project those qualities. That's why she usually keeps a couple of bottles of the garnet-colored liquid on hand (instant "je ne sais quoi").

Finally, wine has another really nice feature—it gets you hammered! When I drink alcohol, I *always* get sexually excited. Over the years, I've found that I start feeling the tingly effects about five minutes after my second big sip. Once I recognized this systematic occurrence, I coined the term "second-sip tingle" to describe what I was feeling to my friends. There's no doubt that wine gets people in the mood to boogie. Why else would men work so hard at getting women drunk? There is a great payoff (sex) if their plans work—and they usually do. Everyone knows, though, that too much wine will cause one to lose her senses. It's not particularly appealing to a would-be lover when a woman is making a fool of herself by slurring her words, falling off her chair, or stripping off her clothes in public. A DD saves those sacred acts only for strangers at Mardi Gras.

You walked into a singles' party dressed to kill. You mingled and drank for while. Suddenly, you went from being sophisticated to intoxicated. After you got a few numbers and caught a ride home from one lucky single, you realized your new dress had red wine stains all over it. As soon as you walk through your door, pop open a bottle of white, and apply some to the stain. Then, soak the stain in cold water for 20 minutes. Next, rub some salt onto the discolored area, and rinse with more cold water. If this doesn't work, try to drink only white wine or vodka tonics from now on. Finally, leave your dress to dry and go entertain the guest you brought home from the singles' party.

5) *Grass/Flowers:* If you like to roll in the hay, you might be a Dirty Diva. Like so many other DDs, I like to get close to nature and do lots of natural things. Those things include exercisin' the ferret, greasin' the weasel, goin' huntin', and gettin' jack in the orchard. Doin' any of these activities puts your good clothes at risk for grass 'n flower stains, I reckon. Expect that if you're goin' stargazin' on your back, you'll have to clean up more than just an ordinary cum stain, darlin'. Them grass stains be harder to get out than a duck stuck in mud.

Gently rub the grass stain with a baby's toothbrush and regular toothpaste. Next, rinse with cold water. Repeat until the stain is removed, and launder as usual. Make sure the stain is completely eliminated before you launder, or else everyone on the farm is gonna see them thar stains on your knees.

6) *Hair:* If you're like me, you trim your own pubes in your own bathroom. Sure, some Dirty Divas like to get waxed clean by a complete stranger at the spa, but that's not as dirty as doing it yourself over a trash can with your man's clippers. Besides, he'll be intoxicated by the scent during his morning shave!

Use a lint roller to clean hair that has fallen onto the bathroom floor. Lint rollers were designed to pick up cat hair. Why not pussy hair too? A broom and dustpan are not effective because the large bristles of the broom can't manage the tiny, fine hairs. Not to mention the fact that once swept by the broom, those tiny hairs usually end up pushed under the dustpan, not in it.

Should you foolishly decide to trim your tuft over your bedroom carpet, you have no choice but to vacuum and then use the lint roller. Try not to trim over carpet because your hairs will get trapped between the carpet fibers, which will cause bacteria to grow.

7) ***Ink (including copier toner):*** Any DD who has ever worked in an office realizes the importance of this section. You have probably escorted your clients into the company copy room to collate files dozens of times. Most of the time, all is normal—you give your clients their freshly copied files, and they go on their merry way. Other times, one thing leads to another; you lock the door and overcome your client's objections in a very unprofessional way. Of course, you don't want the others in

the office to catch on. So, it's imperative that after a good funch on the community copier you are able to remove the incriminating toner stains on your clothes. After all, your colleagues don't need to know how you landed the Anderson account.

Soak the stain in cold water for 10 minutes. Next, brush baking soda into the stain with a baby's toothbrush. Let the mixture sit on the stain for 45 minutes, and then rinse with cold water. Repeat until the stain is removed, and launder as usual. If this doesn't work, apply rubbing alcohol to the stain, and rinse with cold water. Then, launder as usual.

8) *Lubes (including gels, liquids, and lotions):* Don't you hate it when you're getting your bean flicked and you just can't get wet? It's even worse if the flicker doesn't stop! Vigorous rubbing without lubrication leaves you turned off with an inflamed bean—the most frustrating feeling in the entire world. Although I am always excited during foreplay, I sometimes remain as dry as the Sahara. So, what am I to do? I break out the lube! Although some are uncomfortable admitting it, personal lubricants are sometimes needed to properly grease the gash. We've got warm lube. We've got flavored lube. We've even got spermicidal lube. So many lubes, so little time.

I was never accustomed to using personal lubricants until I started dating a particular guy. He had been using lube for years to give himself treats. Once he introduced me to the slippery stuff, I was sold. Instantly, I felt less self-conscious knowing that I didn't have to stop the fun once I became dry.

Having automatic moisture allowed me the freedom to concentrate on other, more important things.

Because I use lube so frequently, I've had to clean it out of almost everything I own. If you are an enthusiastic user of artificial splooge, then you will need to know how to clean the stains it creates.

Remove any excess lube from the material, and blot the stain with hot water. Then, work some liquid laundry detergent into the stain, and rinse under a running stream of hot water. Launder as usual. If the lube has dye in it, see the "Jell-O" section.

9) *Makeup:*

a) *Blush, eyeliner, eye shadow, foundation, and mascara:*
When I prepare for a date, I take great pleasure in getting ready. For me, primping is extremely therapeutic. I am in an incredibly relaxed state, working towards only one goal, making myself as desirable to my date as possible. I usually take a nice, long, hot shower. Then, I slather myself in lotion and wrap myself in a cozy robe. I listen to good jazz and drink vintage wine while I put on my face. Making sure my application is flawless, I take my time preparing my facial masterpiece. After I'm satisfied with my work, I get dressed and hope that all my efforts are in vain. I want nothing more than to see my hard work smeared on a pillowcase by the end of the night.

I'm a nuzzler—I love to rub my face and body all over my lover. Oftentimes, I find myself nuzzling my lover before he even gets a chance to undress! If you're like me and you wear makeup, at some point, you've probably noticed your face paint on a pair of pants or a blouse. If you haven't caught on to long-wearing makeup yet, you'll need to know how to clean these stains off valuables.

The best way to remove makeup is with ... makeup remover. Always use an oil-free version or you'll end up with an oil stain in addition to the blush or foundation you're trying to eliminate. Apply some makeup remover to the stain, rub gently, and rinse with warm water. Launder as usual.

b) ***Lipstick:*** You have to attend a conference in Chicago. You hop the plane, and you're off. A few hours later, you're checking into a fabulous hotel and preparing for your seminar. Day turns to night, and the next thing you know, you're stuck listening to some insipid lecture while the buzzing city beckons to you. You gaze out the window at the shimmering skyline and wonder how you can make your escape. There are so many other things you'd rather be doing than listening to this stuffed shirt drone on about quality control. Suddenly, the shirt's voice is nothing more than static, and your eyes meet a stranger's across the room. You think to yourself, "Well, look what we've got here!"

Your evening is shot when you learn of the required 7 a.m. meeting the next morning, so you just decide to call it a night. Later, you can't sleep, so you get dressed and go to the hotel bar. The stranger from the seminar walks in. You never drop his penetrating gaze as he walks closer. Finally, he reaches your table, and he's so close you can almost taste his musky cologne. Hours pass. You're confident, sparkling, and riveting. You're on fire. He's classy, gorgeous, and captivating. He's ... he's ... married!

There's nothing you or your married lover wants less than to have his wife discover your lipstick stain on his collar. If she learns what's going on between you and her man, you forfeit a regular hot beef injection, and he forfeits half of his estate. You both have a lot riding on this.

Apply an oil-based (make sure it's not oil-free) makeup remover to a lipstick stain, and rub it between your fingers. Next, rub liquid dish soap into the stain, and rinse with warm to hot water. Repeat these steps until the stain is removed, and launder as usual. The Mrs. won't ever have a clue.

Here's a secret I'd like to share with you: invest in some long-wearing lipstick. The absolute best brand is Max Factor's LipFinity. It is amazing—it won't wear off even after hours of lip service. After trying it, you'll be pleased to find that the likelihood of ruining expensive garments is practically eliminated.

I must warn you, however, to avoid *vigorous* contact between the LipFinity and clothing. I learned the hard way. Once, I was teasing a man with my mouth on the bulge of his pants, and he was left with a big red ring on his crotch. It was such an inconvenience for us because we were in the car on the way to visit some friends. Eventually, we had to turn around so he could change his pants. He also had to put them through the wash about five times before the ring came out.

c) **Nail polish:** Does your foot-worshipping boyfriend like to kneel down before you to paint your toes while you, coldly ignoring him, file your nails? Yeah, I'm not into that either, but lots of DDs really enjoy the whole domination thing. Let's face it; lots of daisies insist that you play the dominant role even though you'd rather be the equal or subordinate one.

Never in my life did I think that nail polish could be such an orgasm instigator until I started dating that guy with the foot fetish. At first, I found it novel to be objectified for my feet instead of my tits or my ass, but soon, it got really old. What started out as requests that I step on his chest and maliciously order him around quickly became requirements. Soon, the dumb fuckhead couldn't even cum without my foot in his face! After a while, he wouldn't even bother to entertain my sexual needs. Where's the fun for me? You know a Dirty Diva doesn't stick around to please a guy at her expense, so I was outta' there. Unfortunately, "Foot Fucker" left nail polish stains all over my sofa throw because he was not only selfish, but also sloppy.

Pull the fabric taut around a glass (with the stain over the mouth of the glass), and fasten with a rubber band. Slowly trickle nail polish remover with a small dropper onto the stain. Repeat until removed. You may be left with a dye stain after the nail polish is removed. If you are, apply a mixture of equal parts hydrogen peroxide and water to the stain, and allow it to sit in the sun until the dye is removed. Now, I paint my own nails.

10) ***Mud/Dirt:*** Is there anything dirtier than dirt? There couldn't possibly be! If dirty didn't mean dirty, we'd be saying, "Clean your face. You look so grassy!"

Lots of women like to feel dirty when they're fooling around because they make the association that dirty is bad. We like to feel like bad girls because it's more fun than being good.

Could this be why mud wrestling is so popular? Mud is certainly messy (dirty), and the act of wrestling is certainly aggressive (bad). Mud wrestling may just be the perfect combination of dirty and bad. No wonder so many women participate in it and so many men like to watch it. Women get to feel like they're bad girls who need taming, and men get to feel like they have a shot at taming those bad girls. Lesbyterians, on the other hand, get the best of both worlds—they can be the bad girls and at the same time try to tame the other bad girls. With mud wrestling, there's something for everyone!

Before I die, I feel that in order to fulfill my obligations as the queen of Dirty Divas, I must mud wrestle. I can't purport to be dirty unless I'm willing to take on all that being dirty entails. Although I've never actually gone to a mud-wrestling event, I have wrestled around in the mud outside with a guy or six. Each time, I was able to restore my clothes to their original condition. First, I made sure to go rump splitting for an extra 45 minutes in a dry place so that the mud on my clothes could harden. Then, I scraped the hard pieces off and applied a mixture of equal parts rubbing alcohol and warm water. Finally, I laundered as usual.

11) Odors (including body, fecal, food, perfume, and urine):

Mmm ... smells like sex in here. Forget Shalimar. Where can I find bottled Essence of Schtup?

Don't you love the earthy smell of sex? It's such a rich and intense aroma. Sometimes it's a bit sweet, but it's not at all floral. While the smell is definitely pungent, it's not quite bitter. It's neither particularly good nor particularly bad. There's just no other smell in the world like it (which would explain why you can't get it in a bottle). Also, the smell of sex varies among couples—different bodies emit different fragrances, as you learned in the "Perspiration" section. It's difficult to describe the smell, but there's no mistaking the aroma of freshly fucked freaks.

Because there's no question as to how sex smells, it's crucial that you are able to eliminate the odor before your affairs quickly become public knowledge. Also, your smell on her husband's shirt is the first indication (besides a lipstick stain) to your married lover's spouse that he is cheating. To avoid causing strife in an otherwise happy marriage, you must eradicate any trace of your essence on your lover's person.

Trying to eliminate a perfume aroma with perfume is not the brightest thing to do, so don't do it. Sprinkle a bit of baking soda on a damp cloth, and apply to the most heavily scented areas of the fabric until the aroma is gone. If you use this technique, no one will know that you and your lover just did the four-legged frolic.

12) *Oil/Grease*: See the "Oil/Grease" entry in the "Food/Drink" section.

13) *Paint*: While sitting on a park bench, you and your girlfriend are groping each other's glands. Suddenly, you realize that there are white stripes all over your little black dress. Then, you notice the fallen "Wet Paint" sign on the ground next to the bench. At first, you're very peeved, but soon things start to get more intense with Cindy, and the two of you decide to dive into the bushes (in the bushes), out of public view. You discard your stained dress so that Cindy can start eating your flowers.

Never let paint dry on your clothes! You will find that hardened paint is almost impossible to remove. In the aforementioned account, I was so overcome with horniness that I didn't act quickly on the paint stains—I acted quickly with Cindy.

When I got home, it was too late to salvage my dress. If you are ever in this precarious situation, you will need to make a decision—which is more important, your clothes or your cooch?

For water-based paint stains, soak the spot in cold water. Next, apply some laundry detergent to the spot, and rub vigorously. Finally, launder as usual. For oil-based paint stains, apply turpentine to the spot, and rinse with warm water. Next, apply some laundry detergent to the spot, and rub vigorously. Finally, rinse in hot water, and launder as usual.

14) *Soot:* "Ho! Ho! Ho!" Who you callin' a ho, bitch? You callin' me a ho? Oh. Okay, Santa, I just wanted to make sure.

Do you like to date guys who dress up as Santa Claus and go chimney sliding? I can't be the only one with the St. Nick fetish, can I? Men enjoy role-playing too. How could a man not like pretending to be a jolly fat man who comes to you in the middle of the night bearing a special present? Because every man thinks his package is the *ultimate* present, playing Santa Claus is more popular with the guys than you might think.

After "Santa" slides down my chimney, I ask him if he's brought me anything for being a good girl. He says that he knows I haven't been a good girl because he's seen me when I'm sleeping (not always at home) and knows when I'm awake (until the wee hours of the night). But, he makes a concession. He says that even though I've been bad, he'll give me a present if I promise to be better. I agree and decide that getting my chimney swept again would be the most satisfying present for me. He obliges and gives me the gift that only bad girls get.

The next morning, after Santa has gone, I notice black scuffs all over the carpet and furniture because the "Jolly One" neglected to take off his sooty clothes the night before.

Make a mixture of equal parts baking soda and warm water. Apply the mixture to the stain with a lint-free cloth, and blot dry. If this doesn't work, sprinkle baking soda directly to the stain, and rub with a damp cloth. Launder as usual. Saint Patrick's Day is right around the corner! Now that you're done playing with Santa, perhaps you can find time for a special little leprechaun. P.S. He's not as little as you might think!

15) *Tree sap:* A DD can't get much dirtier than when she's getting pronged up against a tree in the middle of Central Park—unless, of course, she's on her way to a date with someone other than the guy pronging her against the tree. Man, was my leg dirty!

Tree sap is hard as fuck to remove. Try to remove any excess with a blunt edge. Pretend you're marinating some meat; apply canola oil to the sap, and allow it to rest for one full day. Then, rinse the stain with rubbing alcohol. Next, pretreat with liquid laundry detergent, and launder as usual. If this doesn't work, give up, and save this garment for future tree-fucking transactions.

16) *Wax (including candle):* I was first introduced to using melted candle wax for play when I was at a BD/SM party in DC. At this party, there were different booths set up for different sex-play preferences. For instance, there were booths that promoted spanking, girl-on-girl action, dick piercing, blindfolded play, whipping, foot worshipping, and many other intriguing subjects.

Amidst the screams coming from the dick-piercing booth, I noticed the candle-wax section. Most participants were instructed to lie on their stomachs (naked) while the booth administrator proceeded to drip melted wax all over their backs. Because they were lying on their stomachs, there was no way for them to know when and where the wax would fall next. The participants would unleash gratified shudders each time a dollop of wax would fall from the candle onto their backs. Some would even let out little moans, suggesting to the administrator that his work was thoroughly appreciated.

In the end, each waxed participant left the table with a tender pink back, completely satisfied. (See "Burn marks" and "Ice cream" sections.)

The next time you plan to get your nipples scalded by a dripping taper, have some store-bought wax remover on hand. I was able to get candle wax out of the mosquito netting around my bed with Goo Gone—it worked like magic. Just follow the directions on the bottle.

17) *Wood/Furniture polish*: Dirty Divas leave no stone unturned and no table uncundied. With that sacred rule in mind, the furniture in the DD's home is sure to see lots of action and need frequent cleaning. It could get really messy if you and your partner don't wait before waxing on the furniture you've just polished. Your clothes will reap the consequences.

The last time Gregory came over, I had prepared a nice meal for him. I greeted him in my satin robe at the door. Why bother dressing when the clothes will just come off? We had a delicious dinner, and I cleared the table, but Gregory was hungry for more. I was sitting seductively on my dining room buffet table when I suggested that he have something healthy because we'd just had such a rich meal. He said that I read his mind, and he opened my robe to help himself to the curly greens.

The next evening, I got to work cooking a beautiful dinner for Sam. Everything was in order, so I climbed the stairs to my bedroom so that I could put a final coat of lotion all over my body. I slathered on the rich scented cream, put on my satin robe (the one I had worn the night before), and descended the staircase. I caught a glimpse of myself in the mirror on the way down and noticed oily stains on my robe. I couldn't figure out how I had gotten them, but then I remembered that I had served myself to Gregory on the freshly polished buffet the evening before. I realized that the oily stains were from the furniture polish I used on my buffet. When Gregory was having the curly greens, I neglected to take off my robe.

I knew that Sam was due in less than an hour, so I had to act swiftly to eliminate the oily wood-polish stains. First, I applied a little canola oil to the stain and allowed it to penetrate for 15 minutes. Next, I rubbed dishwashing liquid (shampoo also works) into the stain. Then, I ran it under a stream of hot water. Finally, I applied some liquid laundry detergent directly to the stain, waited 10 minutes, and laundered as usual. Sam finally arrived, and he commented how sexy my robe looked on me. All my hard work paid off: I got lucky—again.

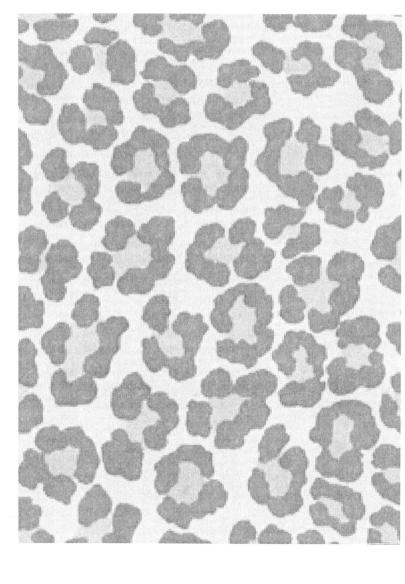

6

CLOSING

WE DIRTY DIVAS ARE living in a very oppressive and hypocritical society. It's socially unacceptable for a woman to enjoy her sex life (unless *Sex and the City* becomes a living reality). Thus, we are forced to remain silent about our preferences. Men's sexual desires, on the other hand, are held in very high regard. Everywhere we look, there are beer commercials, magazines, prescription drugs, and advertisements all geared towards men's sexual pleasure. What about us? Why aren't there more commercials with scantily clad men? Why did it take so long for a female sexual dysfunction pill to come out after Viagra? What about our sexual desires? If you've ever made any of these queries, chances are society's answer has been "You are sexually insignificant!" Why? Because we are women. If we can't be indulged simply because we are women, then I pose the following questions: Hath not a woman eyes? Hath not a woman hands, sexual organs, sexual dimensions, affections, passions? According to society, the answer is still a resounding "No!"

Because we don't like it when others tell us what we can and can't do, some of us may get up in arms. Once we've had enough of the double standard, we may even rebel by doing "dirty" things: we'll be vocal about our sexual preferences or, heaven forbid, have sex on the first date! Immediately after any action we take, we feel empowered, invincible. We start to believe that we are equal to men and that the hypocrisy is lessening because we are revolutionizing the world through our actions. For a short time, we are even led to believe that because civilization is evolving and becoming more progressive, our behavior will be condoned. In fact, many men will even tell us that they think we're "strong" or "independent," actually encouraging our behavior. Soon though, those praises become cautions; you'll be told that you're "wild" or "dangerous." It doesn't take long before you've become "slutty" or "skanky." This is manipulation. Our mothers (and those who love us) tell us to keep quiet about our sexuality because they know that this manipulation is inevitable. They also know that those people who are publicly

CLOSING

empowering us may even believe we are completely warranted in our actions, but because of cultural programming, they eventually recant. Undoubtedly, societal pressure can destroy the lives and reputations of those who speak out against collective opinion, so it's much safer and easier to conform. Ultimately, our initial supporters succumb to the pressure and abandon their controversial beliefs; that is why even the most liberal-appearing people will turn out to be the harshest critics of those of us who justifiably exploit our sex appeal.

In general, our sexual freedom is affected by what society propagates. Society says that we have to give it up to men for their sexual pleasure but that when we want a little action, we require chastising. When we spread our legs, we're called sluts. When we shut them, we're called prudes. Can we ever win? Yes, we can. We can empower ourselves by insulating one another from society's pressure. How? We need to consort and confer with like-minded women who will accept us and reinforce our importance. Owning this manual is a step in the right direction; it helps you to realize that there are others like you.

Whether you consult this guide from time to time, very often, or every day, you're a Dirty Diva! As a DD, you owe it to your sisters to share this information. Some women feel embarrassed to talk about sex-induced messes because society looks down upon women who are candid about their sex lives. The shame and guilt need to stop. Now is the time to take action! Take it upon yourself to mentor all the others like you. Your fellow DDs will empower themselves by using this guide and employing it as a practical, everyday reference.

Every comrade we gain is another step toward acceptance. With every DD we embrace, we will gain more credence. Indeed, each time we welcome another sister, we will become more tolerant and thereby tolerated.

There is no time like the present! Join the Dirty Diva revolution! Spread the word—and then, your legs.

ABOUT THE AUTHOR

Laura Goodman lives an anonymous life just outside Baltimore, Maryland. She is the branch manager of a mortgage company and has been successfully eliminating sex-induced stains since she was 15 years old.